Essential Business Coaching

Essential Business Coaching offers a much-needed answer to the question of what makes a good business coach.

The authors draw on 60 years of combined experience to provide an in-depth review of best practice and theory. They provide a thorough examination of the changing nature of work, the need for new sources of competitive advantage and the benefits of investing in coaching. Useful ideas for further reading are found throughout, along with numerous examples of real business coaching situations. The inclusion of interviews with both corporate sponsors and individual clients provides a unique insight into what makes good coaching in practice.

The combination of solid theory and abundant examples make *Essential Business Coaching* an invaluable tool for all business coaches as well as counsellors, psychotherapists, human resource professionals and senior managers.

Averil Leimon is a partner at White Water Strategies, a London-based consulting firm. She has pioneered the process of coaching in business for over 20 years.

François Moscovici is co-founder of White Water Strategies. His career as a strategy consultant, business manager, in-house mentor and executive coach has mainly been with companies such as Thorn EMI and PricewaterhouseCoopers.

Gladeana McMahon is a leading personal development and executive coach. She is a Vice-President and Fellow of the Association for Coaching and a Fellow of the British Association for Counselling and Psychotherapy.

Essential Coaching Skills and Knowledge

Series editors: Gladeana McMahon, Stephen Palmer and Averil Leimon.

The *Essential Coaching Skills and Knowledge* series provides an accessible and lively introduction to key areas in the developing field of coaching. Each title in the series is written by leading coaches with extensive experience and has a strong practical emphasis, including illustrative vignettes, summary boxes, exercises and activities. Assuming no prior knowledge, these books will appeal to professionals in business, management, human resources, psychology, counselling and psychotherapy, as well as students and tutors of coaching and coaching psychology.

Titles in the series

Essential Business Coaching
Averil Leimon, François Moscovici & Gladeana McMahon

Achieving Excellence in Your Coaching Practice
Gladeana McMahon, Stephen Palmer & Christine Wilding

Essential Business Coaching

*Averil Leimon,
François Moscovici and
Gladeana McMahon*

Routledge
Taylor & Francis Group

LONDON AND NEW YORK

First published 2005
by Routledge
27 Church Road, Hove, East Sussex, BN3 2FA

Simultaneously published in the USA and Canada
by Routledge
270 Madison Avenue, New York, NY 10016

Routledge is an imprint of the Taylor & Francis Group

© 2005 Averil Leimon, François Moscovici & Gladeana McMahon

Typeset in New Century Schoolbook by
Keystroke, Jacaranda Lodge, Wolverhampton

Printed and bound in Great Britain by Biddles Ltd, King's Lynn
Paperback cover design by Lisa Dynan

This publication has been produced with paper manufactured to strict
environmental standards and with pulp derived from sustainable forests.

British Library Cataloguing in Publication Data
A catalogue record for this book is available from the British Library

Library of Congress Cataloging in Publication Data
Leimon, Averil.
Essential business coaching/by Averil Leimon,
François Moscovici, and Gladeana McMahon.
p. cm. – (Essential coaching skills and knowledge)
Includes bibliographical references and index.
ISBN 1-58391-882-5 (hbk) – ISBN 1-58391-883-3 (pbk)
1. Executive coaching. 2. Mentoring in business.
I. Title: Business coaching. II. Moscovici, François.
III. McMahon, Gladeana, 1954– IV. Title. V. Series.
HD30.4.L45 2005
658¢.07124–dc22   2005008209

ISBN 1-58391-882-5 (hbk)
ISBN 1-58391-883-3 (pbk)

Contents

Preface

Coaching has rapidly become one of those words which crops up in every context. It even features in popular television shows where once counsellors and psychotherapists were the butt of humour. Everyone who is anyone now has a coach. Anyone who might fancy a change of career thinks about becoming a coach. Why not? It is a wonderfully satisfying and sometimes lucrative profession to be in. Coaching, like most good things, can be a very simple and highly effective process. It is a joy to behold when results are stunning. We should not settle for anything less.

Another book on business coaching?

What could justify yet another book on coaching when there are so many already available? Many tell you how to become a coach and offer sensible approaches and sophisticated tools. However, if you google 'business coaching books' you get about 2 million answers and, despite this plethora of riches, we feel that our profession is in a state of flux and in danger of confusing itself and its clients. Specifically, we think that a mature industry should be able to answer the following simple questions:

- Objectively, what makes a good business coach? What science do they use? How do they reconcile apparently conflicting objectives of sponsor and client? Do coaches need to be psychologists, business people or both? What is quality?
- Objectively, what do business coaching clients want? How do they choose their suppliers? Have they been happy with their

experience? How do they measure return on investment? Have individual clients found business coaching significantly helpful and worth the effort? Which approaches work best for them?

This book is therefore about raising objectivity, both in the eye of the coach and that of the client (both buyer and user). More specifically, we will cover the following areas.

Clarifying the offering and the value

The coaching profession has mushroomed to provide this service. The result is a continuum from the vaguely ineffectual to the potentially downright dangerous with some excellent, sound professional offerings somewhere along the line. This book aims to clarify and develop professional and productive standards before there is a swingeing backlash against an ill-defined group of people who just happen to use the same descriptor. We also believe that it is wrong for coaches to offer merely an emotional blanket to their clients and not aim for business results every time.

A science and an art

The scientific part of coaching tends to be forgotten as its practitioner base widens and coverage becomes more popular. We aim to demonstrate which elements of cognitive, behavioural and positive psychology are essential to the practice of sound business coaching. We also want to show how business coaches who are not formally trained as psychologists can acquire a robust grounding in the science of the mind.

This book will explore the specialist skills required to be a business coach. At its most basic this involves adding value not just to the individual but also to the organisation. Unlike other forms of coaching, the business coach is required to balance the needs of the individual with the demands of a profit-oriented organisation. Successful business coaches are more likely to require an understanding of and have experience in business itself than coaches in other fields. They may also be required to monitor expectations and outcomes in line with company goals. So we will spend some time on the art of weaving-in psychological science to help businesses get their results.

Facts, more facts and strong opinions

If you are looking for a manual of coaching and two-by-two diagrams, read no further. This book is concerned with facts ahead of concepts, although we provide frameworks and road-maps. We are focused on sharing best practice so that readers can apply it to their own context. Three things define best practice: first, what clients tell us. We have interviewed five multinational companies on their purchasing practices and had candid conversations with them on what works and what doesn't. We have also interviewed five individual clients, to gain insight into the specific results they were after and to see if and how they obtained them.

The second element of best practice is an objective measure regarding the return on the investment in business coaching. We have worked with the Association for Coaching to find objective data and report the latest findings on the subject.

The last component of best practice is our expert opinion: collectively we have over 60 years of experience as business coaches, clinical psychologists, business advisers, market analysts and professional communicators. We have many war stories to share and are fairly judgemental on what works and what doesn't. We are also addicted to science: before we adopt a new 'technology', we want to see the academic research, the statistical proof, the peer reviews and then we test it ourselves.

So this book will challenge complacency. It will demand high standards of professionalism and will eschew the mere competency of some coaching. The aim will be to inspire people with the excitement of the changes possible through effective coaching. If it were not plagiarism, it could be called *The Joy of Coaching*.

Who are we?

Averil Leimon

Averil started her career in Glasgow, first in the NHS, then setting up the first private psychology practice in Scotland. Over the years she has developed a vast array of research-based tools to transform individuals and teams in manufacturing and service industries. Her work initially focused on stress, handling difficult people and professional communication. She also developed a new approach to coaching senior management in behaving like coaches themselves at companies like Polaroid, HP, Unilever and Reuters. Averil was recently chosen as one of the UK's top ten coaches by the *Independent on Sunday* and is one of the first UK-based psychologists qualified in the academic field of positive psychology. Averil is a partner at White Water Strategies, a London-based consulting firm and her current clients include many of those interviewed for this book (more details can be found at wwstrategies.com).

'For over 20 years, I have pioneered the process of coaching in business. (It wasn't even called coaching at first). I have coached both individuals and teams in all market sectors towards a variety of business goals. My background in clinical psychology gave me a great advantage in understanding how people think, feel and change. During this time the pace of change, the turbulence of the markets, the ups and downs have all necessitated flexibility in approach. Most recently, the emergent field of positive psychology as a distinct branch of academic psychology has mirrored the approaches I have taken to enable people to achieve not just their potential but also a meaningful life. Psychological techniques and approaches can greatly enhance the efficacy of any coach.'

François Moscovici

François has been in turns a strategy consultant, a business manager, an in-house mentor, an executive coach and an entre-preneur. He has worked in most industries as an adviser and operator, from small companies to blue chips such as Thorn EMI and PwC. He is the co-founder of White Water Strategies and brings a unique understanding of both business issues and what coaches need to do to be credible in a corporate environment. His current research focuses on 'the first 100 days': how to make newly-appointed executives more successful and faster through business coaching.

'Business is always looking for sources of competitive advantage and I have spent all my career demystifying and implementing the Next Big Thing: be it privatisation or European integration or electronic business. The long-term motivation of management and the ability to deliver the strategy is clearly the challenge of the next ten years. Coaching is a wonderful approach, as long as your client trusts your business judgement and you can switch your own expertise on or off at will.'

Gladeana McMahon

A leading personal development and executive coach, Gladeana provides coaching and therapy to politicians, celebrities, senior business people and those in the media. She was also listed as one of the UK's top ten coaches by the *Independent on Sunday*. A regular broadcaster, her media work includes being co-presenter of Granada Television's five-part series *Sex and Soaps*, appearances on Channel 5's *Britain's Worst Parent*, ITV2's *Curse of Reality TV* and Channel 4's *Big Brother*. She helped develop a variety of activities for BBC1's 25-part series *Life's too Short*. Gladeana is the GMTV life coach, the stress coach for the Channel 4 website and currently writes a weekly column for the women's section of the *Daily Express*.

Gladeana is an internationally published author with 16 books of an academic and self-help nature. She is a Vice-President and Fellow of the Association for Coaching and a Fellow of the British Association for Counselling and Psychotherapy. She is also an accredited counsellor and cognitive-behavioural psychotherapist and Co-Director of the Centre for Stress Management and Centre for Coaching. She is Head of Coaching for Fairplace plc.

'I combine academic rigour with down-to-earth communication skills. I have an informed and direct approach, with humour and compassion being my trademarks. My motto is, *"Don't say, 'I can't.' Say, 'How can I?'"* and I believe it too.'

Who is this book for?

Business coaching is unique because the sponsor, the funder and the user are generally different people. It gets even more interesting because some buyers such as HR professionals can also be practitioners; managers can be sponsors, users and also practitioners with their own staff. Finally, business coaches can come from inside the business itself (in which case they can adopt all roles!) as well as from the outside, and they may well be managers of businesses themselves . . .

These are the benefits that each can expect.

HR professionals

HR professionals should find the objective data as well as the anecdotes provided by peers and clients of great interest: it will help them define coaching programmes and set expectations for sponsors and funders.

If they also act as internal coaches for their organisations, they will find the book useful to specify the nature of their role, define the scope of their business coaching and determine where their boundaries should lie.

Business managers

Managers should welcome examples of best practice and contrast it with their own experience if they have already been at the receiving end of coaching. The book will also help them translate the coaching process to staff they sponsor.

Forward-thinking managers who want to develop a more modern coaching style of management instead of the traditional command and control approach will benefit from contemplating which new approaches, skills and attitudes they can learn.

Obviously, managers who wish to establish their objectives and standards prior to commissioning suppliers will find the book useful when they establish their baseline requirements for professional coaching standards.

Coaching professionals

Finally, both tutors and students of coaching will benefit from both the skills development and the insight into current business settings and trends. We obviously welcome their questions, comments and constructive criticism!

Contents

So, how do we achieve our lofty objectives?

Essential Business Coaching begins with an **introduction** to the concept of coaching in general and in business specifically. We examine the changing nature of work, the need for new sources of competitive advantage and how investing in coaching can help. We also review the various ways to measure return on investment.

Chapter 2 looks at the **theoretical framework** of coaching. We map a continuum from counselling to coaching and mentoring, distinguishing differences and highlighting common skills. Distinctions such as business versus executive coaching are examined. We review various models of coaching and propose a simple and practical framework.

Chapter 3 carefully examines the most effective **techniques** used in business coaching. We also identify the beliefs and attitudes essential for excellent results. As we explore our preferred framework, we make reference to a variety of **psychological disciplines** that may not have been accessible to coaches coming from non-psychological backgrounds.

Chapter 4 considers the **specific applications** of business coaching. We consider three broad themes: business personalities, career stages and coaching for specific business skills. We provide specific insight into successful interventions in areas as diverse as stress, difficult people, coaching women, and selling and presenting.

Chapter 5 focuses on **what corporate clients say** about selecting and using coaches. We report on candid conversations with BT Group, Group 4 Securicor, PricewaterhouseCoopers, Scottish Power and a major European bank. They share with us early experiences, how coaching has evolved and their vision of the future.

Chapter 6 gives a snapshot of coaching in action from the **client's perspective**. Going behind closed doors into the confidential setting of coaching sessions, we give the reader the opportunity to share the experience and get a taste of the extraordinary results that can be achieved as well as of some of the challenges.

Chapter 7 deals with the **professional issues** facing the business coach and suggests solutions. We examine how coaches can raise their professionalism and credibility in business by adopting robust processes such as contracting and confidentiality management. We also consider profession-wide issues including supervision, industry bodies and working with other professionals.

Chapter 8 briefly reviews the lessons learned and considers the **future for business coaching**. It concludes with a set of recommendations and predictions for all involved in our industry: buyers, coaches and professional organisations.

Finally, the **appendices** aim to equip the business coach with useful pro-forma documentation, selected Association for Coaching guidelines and supplementary forms referred to in Chapter 7.

Pre-flight check

The aim throughout this book is to be practical, relevant and as far as possible jargon free. The approach is eclectic and heavily personal. If it is methodologically sound and works, then let's use it in coaching. It is important, especially when working alone in the capacity of coach, to keep replenishing and refreshing techniques and skills, drawing from as many sources as possible. Approaches will be outlined and the emphasis will be on practical application rather than pure theory. We are aware of the mixed audience for this book so, rather than explaining each source and technique in detail, we encourage the reader to make ample use of the bibliography when they want to find out more about a specific subject.

We hope that our book will convince you of the absolute need for excellent, tested, purposeful and respectful coaching and will equip all readers to make it happen in their respective organisations.

Enjoy the journey!

Averil Leimon
François Moscovici
Gladeana McMahon
London, January 2005

1

Introduction: why do we need business coaching?

So what is business coaching and why does it exist? This chapter describes how the business environment has evolved to a stage where coaching has become a source of competitive advantage. It also examines the question of return on investment and takes the view that coaching is probably worth the money spent. The next chapter will deal with definitions, distinctions and questioning frameworks relevant in a business context. At this stage, we will simply argue that business coaching:

- is primarily a process, as opposed to an expertise in content (especially in a business context);
- rests on a deep understanding of how the mind works as well as of the client's context (again, particularly in a business context);
- is never limited to work issues only, even if organisations would prefer it this way; and
- is never purely remedial or 'for stars only'; in particular, the perceptions of the sponsoring organisation may well be very different from the reality of the client; other useful keywords include: solution-focused, collaborative, exploratory and implemented.

Historically, coaching had been used in a business context as a remedial process – now sometimes referred to as *performance coaching*: it was (and still often is) about an individual who did not quite fit the expectations of the business or who had performance or personality 'shortcomings'.

However, as the corporate sector has come to realise the impact of fully utilising and developing its human capital resource, the benefits of ongoing professional development through coaching have become more apparent and desirable. Coaching for excellence assumes that the individual is already fully functioning and successful in what they do. In a rapidly changing corporate environment even the 'star' performer will benefit from having the opportunity to reflect on what works well for them, how to sustain excellence and how to be creative and embrace change in a positive and innovative manner.

The rapid nature of change in society and business has had a major impact on the way that careers are perceived. There is no longer a rigidly defined hierarchy of roles, accompanied by specific training to achieve promotion. Adaptability and flexibility are highly prized yet there is recognition that as humans our natural, spontaneous style of responding to change is often distorted because of erroneous personal beliefs, maladaptive habits or insufficient motivation. Hence coaching has emerged as an accelerated means of learning on the job.

Beyond individual development, organisations have also realised that strategic change programmes are ineffective and fail every time if the people issues – once considered 'soft' issues – are not effectively addressed. The reality of maximising success through people is gradually becoming more than an empty slogan in organisations which need to succeed and recognise that their only competitive advantage comes through giving their people that extra edge.

Loyalty is now a fairly outmoded concept. People move jobs more frequently than in previous generations. This can constitute a haemorrhaging of talent and investment. Coaching enables companies to retain the very best talent by ensuring motivation remains high and development is ongoing. It gives the opportunity to unleash potential and lock in new and productive behaviours.

Our changing business world

Companies do not start to spend money in fairly large amounts on a whim, at least not for sustained periods. In order to understand the attraction of business coaching, it is worth tracking key cross-industry changes of the last 10–20 years. This will also constitute a useful roadmap for the aspiring business coach.

The loss of competitive advantage

Companies are forever looking for new and better ways to compete with one another. The key concept penned by industrial economists is that of 'sustainable competitive advantage' or the ability to generate superior profits over the long term. This can come from any aspect of the business: superior access to distribution, proprietary technology, influence on regulators, cheaper sources of finance, first mover advantage and so on. This search for a better mousetrap is the essence of business and will never go away. However, three phenomena have eroded traditional sources of competitive advantage in the past ten years or so.

Business process reengineering and the accompanying *middle management downsizing* have had a major impact on all industries: there is now a 'best way' of doing things at every level of every industry which is well documented along with an optimal level of costs and staff. This has been reinforced by the widespread adoption of *Enterprise Resource Planning systems (ERPs)*, specialised software that drives the whole company from sales to manufacturing, to delivery and beyond. These systems have been designed around industry best practice, resulting in all major participants in a given industry to adopt similar processes. This has led to major productivity gains but also to a systematic loss of competitive advantage as whole sectors have become more homogeneous.

The next big change has been the emergence of *business process outsourcing*: if a company was not 'best in class' in a given process, then why keep it in-house? New companies emerged who took over whole departments, initially in non client-facing functions such as finance or payroll administration. We currently observe the next phase of this phenomenon with the outsourcing of customer functions such as call centres to India or North Africa (for French speakers). Again, we see whole industries outsourcing the same processes roughly at the same time. This means that the financial performance of various industry participants will improve roughly at the same time: no long-term advantage there.

The *fragmentation of the value chain* has been made possible by the widespread adoption of *cheap and standardised technology*. Few companies today do everything in-house: take for example the supply of domestic electricity: from power generation to transmission to meter reading or sales, the role of the modern electricity distributor is today that of an orchestrator of external suppliers. It may keep in-house core skills such as marketing and billing but it is a very different company from the 'electricity board' of only 15 years ago. We are still far away from the vision of totally disaggregated industries linked through the internet, where buyers and sellers continuously negotiate the best deals, but again there is pressure for each industry to adopt a best practice model based on core capabilities. In other words, where there was previously a single participant in an industry, there are now 10 or 20, each helping to make the industry more competitive, but also more homogeneous.

We are therefore now at a stage where near-instant imitation is possible: companies get their finance from the same global capital markets, they often outsource their manufacturing to the same suppliers and buy their patents from the same global databases. Marketing innovations are identified and copied nearly instantaneously: for example, a few years ago a British supermarket chain heard about a new type of washing powder (capsules) in discussions with a manufacturer and was able to bring its own brand version to market ahead of the original!

So where should sustainable competitive advantage come from? Our view is that *people* represent the last unexploited frontier. The reader may already be convinced, but the point we are making is that the business coach should view their intervention as a way to help create competitive advantage. People are our greatest assets, 'but only when we are growing' should run the subtitle . . . Staff are often seen first and foremost as costs and what is true at the micro level (the need to recruit or retain the best team) often breaks down at the macro level (aggregate costs). Coaching should therefore pay for itself many times over – as we will see below – *and* generate competitive advantage. We would urge the business coach to consider the specific characteristics of their client's industry and think creatively about how to create competitive advantage from having more motivated and effective staff.

The end of apprenticeship

Much has been said and written about multiple careers and the 'war for talent'. The fundamentals are still here: economic growth means that more managers are needed and the desirable management population of 35–45-year-olds will continue to shrink significantly in the next ten years as baby boomers retire. This means that executives expect to be wooed at regular intervals into new careers. The seminal McKinsey article argued that talented executives were attracted by three things: company 'brand' (expressed as culture, values and challenges), an exciting job (autonomy, challenges and advancement) and compensation (relative and absolute pay, location and lifestyle). A business coach has an obvious role to play in improving most of the above and an intervention can usefully be framed both qualitatively and quantitatively as one of the tools of the war for talent.

But if executives change companies regularly, who will invest in their development? Some industries have only a limited interest in developing managers beyond technical training. Investment banking for example is a classic case: owners see no point in developing or retraining when it is just as easy to throw away and replace. However, this does not mean that bankers do not have a need for development. Many end up paying for coaching from their own funds. Beyond this, we see a genuine issue, which we call *the end of apprenticeship*. When staff stayed in companies for 10 or 20 years, there was ample time to develop them both on technical and so-called *soft skills* (those intangible and hard to develop skills that trip many managers as they knock at the boardroom door . . .). Classic careers with plenty of formal development included brand management, commercial banking and management consulting. Others tended to privilege modern forms of apprenticeship, with limited training but plenty of learning by doing: solicitors, hotel managers or journalists, for example.

The business coach has an important role to play in help-ing corporations develop these *humane skills* within the narrower time frame of a fragmented career. Looking at our clients, we see that managers have clearly different needs depending on age and experience: typically managers originate from a specialised area and need help in becoming skilled communicators and people managers. This may be a good time for specific, narrow interventions (e.g. to develop confidence, people handling etc.). As they progress, there is often a need for switching from a specialised delivery role to a more generalist one where influencing and networking skills become more important. Later, having achieved much, some executives may question their long-term role and look for a new challenge. We would encourage business coaches to develop a career-stage focused offering to their clients: it will be easier to sell as a rel-evant investment and the return will be easier to demonstrate to the sponsor.

Is coaching worth the investment?

If companies are going to create competitive advantage by investing in development through coaching, they need to estab-lish whether coaching achieves a decent return on investment (ROI) and if it provides better value for money than other development approaches. The last question is fairly easy to address: as the reader will see in the various interviews (Chapters 5 and 6), coaching is normally one of a range of inter-ventions. The variables to consider are time, cost and the 'direction of the information': the more *content* needs to be delivered from coach to client, the less appropriate one-to-one work is. An essential, although frequently neglected, variable is that of durable change in behaviour: one-to-one is by far the most cost-effective way to design, install and rehearse desired behaviours. Many HR professionals understand this and make coaching part of a blended curriculum. Examples of mixed interventions are discussed in greater detail in Chapter 4.

The vexed question of ROI

ROI is notoriously difficult to measure convincingly for investments in people. One of the authors spent many months analysing the benefits of web-based HR systems (eHR) for corporate clients and came to the conclusion that it was pointless to create sophisticated case studies, as financial analysts could always challenge assumptions (how do you measure the productivity of executives? How do you measure 'speed to uptime' for new recruits?). If even companies notorious for their ability to measure everything, such as Cisco Systems, tell us in interviews that 'after 18 months, it is probably too early to measure ROI in coaching in a meaningful way', what should we do?

Below, we examine several attempts at measuring the value of coaching, including our own, and will let the reader conclude. Our take is that coaching is definitely a worthy investment, *provided that* buyers and clients take the trouble to measure the results. Just because something is difficult to measure doesn't mean that it shouldn't be done!

Research from the Association for Coaching

During the summer of 2004, the Association for Coaching carried out a detailed survey on the ROI of corporate coaching. The results were illuminating for a number of reasons: first they showed that very little objective measurement took place; second that coaching was used to improve personal performance (as opposed to developing teams or linked to a specific project) in 3/4 of the cases, making measurement even more difficult. Only four in ten respondents could confidently point to a quantitative benefit, but almost all reported significant improvement in motivation and people management, with 2/3 willing to be coached again.

The six-to-one rule

A review of the literature on ROI points to a convergence of opinion, particularly in the USA, that coaching pays for itself six times over. Here are some examples:

- In 2001, Metrix Global computed a return of 530 per cent based on 43 interviews at Nortel, or 790 per cent taking into account the impact on staff retention.
- PricewaterhouseCoopers has been using coaching worldwide since 1998 and estimates its return at six to one (*CA Magazine*, March 2004).
- A 2004 survey of 100 coached clients by Manchester Consulting (US) also showed a six times return. Specifically, the biggest tangible business results the coaching yielded were: improved productivity (53 per cent), better quality work product (48 per cent) and greater organizational strength (48 per cent). Intangible benefits were: better relationships with direct reports (77 per cent), better relationships with supervisors (71 per cent), improved teamwork (67 per cent), better relationships with peers (63 per cent), and greater job satisfaction (61 per cent).

The benefit of this six-to-one rule is that even if it is wrong by a factor of three, it still means that coaching earns twice its cost over a short period of time, significantly more than most internal investments a company can make . . .

Basic arithmetic

There are several ways to quantify the potential impact of coaching. Here are two examples derived from our experience.

Coaching has a significant impact on staff retention: successful clients can be restless and think that life would be better elsewhere; conversely clients with development needs might have been isolated by their organisation and be expected to leave. In the UK, replacing a mid-ranking executive costs a minimum of £50,000 (recruitment fees and advertising, excluding indirect costs such as loss of business or HR processes). This means that for each coaching intervention resulting in a legitimate retention there is a direct ROI of five times, assuming a cost of £10,000. On a programme of, say, ten clients resulting in two retentions, you would still get all your coaching money back, excluding any other benefit.

Many ROI surveys talk about increased productivity. This is difficult to quantify but it would be reasonable to expect an increase of productivity of 10 per cent across the board, whatever this might be. If we now expect executives to earn on average £100,000 and to generate three times their direct cost in sales for the company, this means that coaching will have an ROI of three – again for an investment of £10,000 per client. One could take the calculation to gross margin or net earnings, but it is not difficult to make a broad arithmetic case for coaching. The difficulty so far has been to measure the direct impact of coaching on specific people.

In conclusion

Business coaching has a long-term role to play in the world of shorter careers, outsourced processes and instant imitation. Although the industry is still in its infancy and has difficulties making its case to those holding the purse strings, it should be seen as a key means of sustainable competitive advantage. In plain language, happy people are more productive and innovative, and this is what is needed to beat competitors day after day.

We now need to examine the theory and practice of business coaching in order to understand where and how this competitive advantage can be created. This is the object of the next two chapters.

The theoretical framework of coaching

What are we talking about?

Now that we understand the economic context, it is time to turn to definitions and frameworks. This chapter will position business coaching in the range of other person-to-person interventions, review useful models of coaching and propose the simple model to be adopted for the purposes of this book. It will also clarify the essential distinction between *process* and *content* in coaching.

The process of providing definitions can be tedious and many believe that old saying 'you can't describe an elephant but you know what it is when you see one'. Coaching however suffers as a profession from being ill-defined and poorly regulated, so it is worth clarifying what coaching does and does not involve. People still seek to understand the distinction between mentoring and coaching and are at great pains to distinguish coaching from anything which smacks of counselling and all its remedial implications.

Coaching now encompasses a very disparate range of applications from the development of specific skill sets, to personal effectiveness, to presentation, assertiveness or career focus. Business coaching is clearly distinguishable in that the main aim is to produce clear business results for both the individual and the employer. Terms such as 'business' and 'executive' are fuzzy in their use. They may denote the client's level in the hierarchy or be used interchangeably by practitioners. Other labels can also be misleading. The use of the term 'life coach' in itself implies that no one else ever contemplates coaching in terms of the big picture, an obvious fallacy when one pauses to reflect on the links between career success, health and family relationships, for example.

What is coaching? The official view

The Association for Coaching is the UK's main professional association for coaches. It has given a great deal of thought to this issue of definition and description. Below are some direct quotes – a broad selection of the Association's guidelines are available in Appendix 2.

- Coaching enables the client to be the best that they can be in the areas they choose to focus on.
- Typically the client meets with the coach in a one-to-one confidential partnership. The client chooses the focus of the conversation and the coach works with them by listening and contributing observations and questions to help them clarify their understanding of the situation and move them into action to progress towards their goals. (The client brings the content; the coach provides a process, which can apply in any context.)
- Coaching accelerates clients' progress by helping them to focus on where they want to go, to become aware of blocks, attitudes and aptitudes that affect their choices and by supporting them in developing strategies to achieve their goals. Ownership of content and decisions remain with the client throughout.

Perhaps it would be more appropriate to call these examples descriptions rather than definitions.

What distinctions exist between corporate, executive or business coaching? At present they are used fairly indiscriminately within the coaching world. The Association for Coaching has attempted to clarify the nomenclature:

- Corporate or business coaching has been likened to coaching a football team. The coach has corporate goals at heart and may work with individuals or teams to support them in achieving those goals. Coaches need to have an understanding of the operational dimensions of the organisation, although they will focus on the two dimensions of people and leadership.

- Executive coaching is commonly used as a further distinction – sometimes just to denote level in the organisation – that the clients involved will be already executive or identified as high potential managers. The Association makes the distinction that it is up to the executive and their organisation to ensure that the goals of coaching are aligned with the organisation's goals. There is an expectation that the coach should feel as comfortable exploring business-related goals as personal development topics, in order to improve clients' personal performance.

The business coach then, for our purposes, is a highly skilled professional, whose specific specialist knowledge will be about people and their development within organisations. They will have a clear process by which they enter into a relationship with a client. There will also be familiarity, experience and understanding of business settings and how organisations work. As such, we are therefore using the term 'business' in a broad sense to include all other terms such as 'executive' or 'corporate'.

Finally, what is the distinction in business between coaching and mentoring? Again there is confusion within the profession and among clients. All will perhaps become clearer as a more systematic process of training and accreditation is adopted by the profession. We give our own definitions in Table 2.1, but it is worth noting that mentors (providers of expert advice) can benefit tremendously from adopting a *coaching attitude* and honing their coaching skills (described in the next chapter). The mentor, for example, who does not listen but only dispenses advice, will miss valuable opportunities to be instrumental in helping build another's successful career.

Table 2.1 **The expertise continuum**

Role	Relationship	Purpose and style
Mentor	• Elder statesman figure with greater seniority and success • Giving the benefit of experience and contacts. A 'good egg' sounding-board; devil's advocate • One-to-one	• Future long-term career planning • Finding opportunities for exposure and advancement • Usually either outside the organisation or at least not in direct line • Advice giving and directing
Trainer	• Specialist expert • Imparting knowledge and skills • One-to-one or group	• Present-focused • Specific skills acquisition • Instruction, supervised practice and feedback
Business coach	• Equal partnership of two different experts • Joint problem-solving, identifying opportunities, developing skills • Three-way relationship with client and company	• Present and future focus • Leadership development and professional goals • May be internal or external to the organisation • Coaching style
Life coach	• Partnership • One-to-one	• Present and future • Personal goal focus • Coaching style
Counsellor	• Issues or problem focus • Expert driven • Facilitative, non-directive • One-to-one, couple or group	• Past, present and future • Personal psychological distress; resolving personal problems • Usually outside organisation although may work through occupational health • Questioning and listening
Psychotherapist	• Specialist in psychological treatments • Expert-led • One-to-one, couple or group	• Past, present and future • Deeper psychological disturbance • External to the organisation • Range of psychological approaches

The expertise continuum

There are many ways to classify personal development interventions, and two-by-two matrices placing coaching in the top-right corner abound. A simple way is to look at the nature of expert knowledge involved on a dimension from business to psychological. The business coach is sited at a point where there is relative balance between their experience and insight into organisations and into the human condition and capacity for change. The mentor is highly business focused while the psychotherapist is specialised in psychological approaches.

Our view

Business coaching is a very focused one-to-one or group process, the purpose of which is to create learning and achieve change for the professional benefit of the individual and the business benefit of the company. While self-actualisation and a greater sense of satisfaction are important to the individual, they must not be achieved at the expense of achieving clearly defined business results.

The business coach, unlike other coaches, enters into a relationship not only with the individual but also with the client company. Thus, HR professionals and the individual's boss may all be involved in the process. In fact, it is instrumental to success for the business coach to be competent at forming and managing constructive relationships with all parties while guarding confidentiality appropriately and zealously. This can take considerable rigour.

Existing coaching frameworks

Even the most experienced coaches use frameworks. They are starting points from which to build one's preferred version. One of the current illusions of our profession is the tendency towards 'recipe books': that by learning a clever new acronym we will be instantly turned into experienced coaches. When one of us embarked on his coaching career he went to see an ex-colleague who had already developed a successful executive coaching practice and asked him for advice concerning further training. The answer was both reassuring and disturbing: 'you already have all the training you need; simply listen and build on your many years of experience and your own approach will emerge.'

So which frameworks have been used over and over again to create this baseline? There are two big families: those derived from sport and those derived from psychology.

The sports coach legacy

When first starting to review how coaching was being used in organisations, it became apparent that attention, however briefly, should be given to the sporting world. That was where the term 'coach' had come from in the first place. In some organisations where personal development is seen as too fuzzy, a sports-based, competitive metaphor can work wonders to define coaching. One of our clients for example has a training programme called 'refuse to lose', something aligned with the 'drive' dimension of most sports books.

For some of us, sports coaching may conjure the negative image of very bad gym teachers during school days, one of the bullies with megaphones aimed at geeing people up to a good performance. This vision of sports coaching derived from military discipline is no longer used, except perhaps in amateur sports. Today, every professional team has its resident psychologist and coaches have all embraced the themes of flexibility and individuality, as illustrated by the following examples.

Various people had recommended a visit to Ian McGeechan, then coach of the Scottish rugby team. He had also accompanied the British Lions on three tours by that stage. However, most intriguing was the fact that he was mainly recommended because of how he struck people as a person. In an interview with Ian, known as Geech to rugby fans, he talked about the need to develop altruism, forward planning and vision in players. Flexibility and the need to take a longer view were critical. The focus was on playing to individual strengths while forming real team players out of a disparate group of prima donnas. Feedback through 360° and the giving of anonymous attributions ensured that players pointed out each other's best qualities and also gave clear feedback about how their coach was doing. Empathy was vital to the process, he maintained. Because he had once been a player gave initial respect, but the rest had to be earned when coaching for performance. He told a story about team training at RAF Leuchars in Fife, where a NATO exercise had RAF Tornadoes, with two pilots, pitted against the latest US computerised fighter planes flown by a solo pilot. When he asked the RAF pilots how they could possibly compete with such advanced technology, they said, 'There are two of us.' That for him summed up why the need to build in highly effective interpersonal relations could never be described as 'soft' when aiming for dramatic results. Harnessing human talent was not only about physical technical skill. Emotions and relationships were vital considerations.

Sven-Göran Eriksson has been described as 'nothing remarkable', always thinking, always calm, strong in his belief about people's ability. His coaching is again 'nothing remarkable', all about observing, noticing the atmosphere and tuning into how players are feeling at the time. So although sports coaching does not always translate directly to the business field, at these levels there is considerable sophistication in the understanding of how to release the best in already very successful individuals.

How did this increase in sophistication take place? First, because coaches realised the limits of the old ways and second, much credit must be given to Tim Gallwey and his *Inner Game* series of books. He has brought much greater awareness of the complexity of human performance and the need to address not only physical skills acquisition but also the other elements of thought and emotion that interfere with or facilitate achievement.

Let us now turn to the most widely used models of coaching derived from sport.

The COACH model

This is one of the 'second generation' models. It was developed by Don Shula, the legendary NFL coach (six Super Bowl finals, 67 per cent career wins over 33 years as head coach) and Ken Blanchard, co-author of the *One Minute Manager* series. Together they wrote *Everyone's a Coach* in 1995. Their framework is shown in Table 2.2.

This model applied most to those leaders within organisations wanting to coach their teams to better performance.

Table 2.2 **The COACH model**

Letter	Definition	Consequences
*C*onviction-driven	Articulate a vision which is conviction-driven	• Lead by example • Value respect more than popularity • Prize character as well as ability • Enjoy what you do
*O*ver-learning	Practise behaviours until they become second nature	• Limit the number of initiatives • Make people master assignments • Reduce practice errors • Practise continuous improvement
*A*udible-ready	Remain alert to the outside	• How flexible are you? • Does your ego control your decision-making? • How open are you to suggestions from others? • How much do you train those you coach to be ready to change the plan?
*C*onsistency	Manage consequences of behaviour consistently	• Manage consequences • Provide positive consequences • Redirect incorrect performance • Provide negative consequences • Avoid no response
*H*onesty-based	Have intellectual honesty	• Have integrity • Show congruence • Have a sense of humour

Although the labels themselves may seem a bit tortuous (audible-ready? – why not adaptable?), the concepts would have reasonable validity for most coaches. Interestingly, the emphasis is initially on the person coaching rather than the one being coached. As a list of qualities to be aspired to by a coach, it has great value. The implication is that, as these are the qualities essential to good leadership, coaches should be demonstrating them in all their dealings with clients. All the components of good coaching are encapsulated. Business coaching could proceed along these lines to successful outcomes.

It is not however quite a model of the coaching process. It is more about coaching content – the topics that should be covered during the coaching relationship.

The GROW model

This is probably the most widely used framework at present. Sir John Whitmore, both a sportsman and a coach, articulated the findings of Timothy Gallwey in terms that could be understood in a business context. It can be used as a roadmap for both a coaching programme and individual sessions.

Table 2.3 **The GROW model**

Letter	Definition	Example – non-business
G	**Goal** setting for the session, as well as short and long term	• Lose weight • Made explicit: 70kg by Easter
R	**Reality** checking to explore the current situation objectively	• Current weight • Current exercise regimen • Current food intake • Past efforts
O	**Options** and alternative strategies or courses of action	• Subscribe to a slimming programme • Get a personal trainer • Change eating habits • Do it with a friend • Create a reward
W	**What** is to be done, **w**hen, by **w**hom and the **w**ill to do it	• Concrete steps and measurement • Whose support is needed? • Analyse secondary gain of not doing it (e.g. change wardrobe)

Clarifying where we are, where we want to go and options for getting there is essential in coaching. We all benefit from spending time contemplating this for any change we are attempting. The concern here would be if this were only used at a rigid and superficial level. It is usually important to take this a little further and examine some of the reasons we do not always just get on and do things, even with this clarification. How significant are the goals that are presented? Are they aligned with the business goals? How might they have been sabotaged in the past?

The psychological process legacy

Psychology focuses on the growth and development of individuals and on the overcoming of problems. Yet many coaching books do not make clear the relevance of psychological research, principles and techniques to the practice of successful business coaching. As a result many coaches lack a sound comprehensive framework on which to base their approaches and to measure outcomes.

One reason for this must lie in the popular image of psychologists. Beards, couches, reading of minds and psychoanalytic approaches recognisable from Woody Allen films have long held sway. This very narrow definition does not, in fact, reflect past or current reality in a dynamic, change-oriented profession. There are those who would argue that psychology lost its way and became focused on the problems and failures of humanity rather than on tapping into and expanding human potential. Certainly this is the impression gained by the general populace. During the last century psychology achieved a great deal in tackling a range of mental illnesses, which can now be effectively treated. This very success has sometimes made corporate clients wary of being seen to 'psychoanalyse' staff or be besmirched by the implication that there is something wrong with any aspect of the organisation.

However, psychologists may often have been at fault by failing to emphasise how findings and techniques could be put to good use in making more of the human condition. Psychology has not always been good at packaging, sharing and promoting the benefits of its own results. Many successful techniques used in coaching are based on sound psychological research but have only been made accessible through the efforts of disciplines such as neuro-linguistic programming (NLP) which have very successfully encapsulated, labelled and marketed ranges of insights into human relationships and behaviours. For example, it is infinitely more attractive for a layperson to discuss anchoring and its use in advertising than to review data about stimulus-response theory.

So, which models of coaching has psychology given us?

The helping model

Psychology's contribution to coaching frameworks initially came from counselling. The most famous model is the helping model, developed by Gerard Egan (1990) and shown as Table 2.4. Its premise is that clients have problem situations and unused opportunities. The emphasis is initially on complex, confused problem situations that clients have not been able to solve by themselves. However, the model also opens the door to exploring our potential and the notion of client empowerment.

As we see, this approach involves a lot of practical psychology, such as building rapport, using empathy, challenging, reframing, behaviour installation and rehearsal, strategy and trigger identification, creative thinking, visualisation and designing stimulus-response patterns. Obviously, the business culture aspects are missing, but one can see how it created a platform for many counsellors-turned-coaches.

The three-function model

Cole and Bird (2000) developed this as a model of psychology-based communication for medical interviewing. It is now used as a basis for interview training in undergraduate medical schools. We have included it here with minor modifications – see Table 2.5 – as it gives a comprehensive, distilled overview of the phases of a professional relationship and the concomitant skills.

Table 2.4 **The helping model**

Stage	Step	Description
1 Present scenario	The story	Help clients tell their story
	Identify and challenge blind spots	Help clients develop new perspectives on both themselves and their problems
	Search for leverage	Identify what will make a difference and prioritise
	Take action (continuous from then on)	Help client to take action during and between sessions to initiate progress
2 Develop preferred scenario	Preferred scenario possibilities	Visualisation of a problem-free outcome
	Develop viable agendas	Flesh out possible goals and agendas; foresee consequences
	Choice and commitment	Identify incentives that will enable commitment
3 Strategies and plans	Brainstorm strategies for action	Generate a wide range of options
	Choose best strategies	Focus on highest probability of success as opposed to absolutely best outcome
	Turn strategies into plan	Formulate a step-by-step procedure

Our view

Psychology remains the theoretical bedrock of business coaching. If sport was the early analogy, psychology always provided the underlying tool set – which will be described in the next chapter. This was recognised at long last when the British Psychological Society (BPS) established the Special Group in Coaching Psychology in December 2004. The working definition used for the BPS proposal is: 'Coaching Psychology is for enhancing well-being and performance in personal life and work

Table 2.5 **The three-function model**

Function	Objectives	Method	Techniques
1 Relationship	Client to feel: understood, supported, cooperative	Empathic	• Primary impact • Respect • Support • Openness • Non-verbal • Alliance • Last impact
2 Assessment	To achieve comprehensive, reliable, relevant data collection	Exploratory	• Reflective listening • Encourage initial story • Survey issues and priorities • Open questions • Unbiased questions • Review time and agenda • Clarification • Explain any added agenda • Summarise
3 Management	Client to achieve: knowledge, attitudes, behaviour plan	Educational	• Explore • Explain • Probe • Explain • Request • Take home message

domains underpinned by models of coaching grounded in established adult learning or psychological approaches' (adapted from Grant and Palmer 2002). Interestingly, this has already become the third largest subsystem in the BPS.

Psychological science continues to evolve, with new academic disciplines focusing on the well rather than the sick. The positive psychology movement, for example, is receiving substantial funding to develop empirically sound research-based approaches to understanding well-being and character strengths in ways that will enhance performance, meaning and happiness in the relatively normal, untroubled population.

We have chosen to apply psychology in our practices by using what works, what sticks and what is systematic, ethical and demonstrates impact. We call our approach the ITEA model of change.

The ITEA model of change

Our 60 years of coaching and business experience have convinced us that a cognitive-behavioural approach is what works best in business: it addresses the concerns of highly rational managers as well as engaging those – such as entrepreneurs – who are less receptive to an intellectual approach. It generates new behaviours, creating a tipping point when they will become installed as habits. ITEA stands for:

- Impact
- Thought
- Emotion
- Action

Impact – what impact do you have in the situation in question and what impact are these events having on you? Without this self-awareness, change and development cannot happen. Once clients decide that their actions are not necessarily achieving the desired impact on circumstances they can seek to change their thinking and behaviours accordingly. This stage is always the catalyst for change.

Thought – 'There's nothing good or bad but thinking makes it so', as Shakespeare's Hamlet says. Recognising and changing how clients interpret events, by assessing how they filter them through beliefs, values and previous experiences determines their chance of success. Change must occur at these deeper levels to be authentic and sustainable.

Emotion – this is often the overlooked piece of the puzzle. If emotions are a closed book to clients then they do not harness the strongest possible motivation in themselves and others. The research shows that emotional intelligence correlates highly with success. Yet many people have an underdeveloped emotional literacy. They have never learned to measure and classify emotions accurately. As a result, they can be at the mercy of their own emotions and remain amateurs in their dealings with others.

Action – translating all that into sustainable, constructive behaviour change is the ultimate culmination of coaching. Sometimes there may just be better ways of doing things that people have ever thought of. The whole process of coaching allows clients to stand back from their normal life and achieve a sense of perspective not available in the daily turmoil. It is only once destructive assumptions and negative emotions have been cleared that new varieties of creative thinking and problem-solving can enable the client to move out of tunnel vision and experiment with new ways of doing things. By adding a range of professionally honed techniques to their armoury, clients' results improve exponentially.

The ITEA model in action

A recent client, bright, successful and tipped as 'high potential' in his organisation, was seen by others as 'a bit of a rough diamond'. The first stages of the coaching made him aware of these opinions through 360° feedback. His initial tendency was to reject this information and attempt to defend himself. He gradually came to recognise and accept the truth in the observations. It was not his true intention but it was how he came across – i.e. the *impact* he had on others. When his beliefs about the way things should be and his values regarding authenticity were explored, it became clear that he was highly judgemental about those who looked too smooth and political. He rejected development if it meant he had to fake something he knew not to be true. His *thoughts* were challenged and he was required to build up evidence for and against his assumptions rather than blindly believing them to be true. In this way he actively rejected some of his own stereotypes (e.g. he had held fairly parochial and negative views of Americans). This was rather a pity as raising his profile would require work with

American counterparts! By testing his own assumptions and finding a new set of beliefs, he approached this work with professional skill. His *emotions* included discomfort in a range of situations away from the world he knew best. By recognising that many of these feelings were engendered by his negative assumptions, he could change the whole process and take *action* in a very different way, by developing greater sophistication in his communication style with others. Coaching enabled him to see how by asking questions and listening attentively he could both find greater respect for others and build a better professional relationship. A project he has been responsible for globally has produced greater results than anything similar in the company and his passage up the organisation has been endorsed. By embedding these changes so thoroughly in his own distinct personality and core values, the sustainability of the change has been guaranteed.

This process is cyclical. With each new topic raised or experience reviewed the coach is likely to have to work back through each of the areas.

The business coaching process

The ITEA framework for change is not used as a series of isolated loops; it is part of a broader process that covers the coaching relationship between client and coach, but also incorporates the relationship with the sponsoring company. This needs to cover areas such as the needs of the organisation, the transparency of the triangular contract between coach, client and sponsor, the definition of measures of success, the levels of confidentiality and so on. We will expand considerably on why we have chosen this process and how to use it successfully in the next chapter. Its components are:

- Build the relationship
- Draw out the picture
- Achieve change
- Motivate for results
- Conclude the relationship

In conclusion: the need for explicit coaching frameworks

Definitions of business coaching vary enormously and are a sign of the youth of our industry. They remind us about the heated arguments regarding definitions of e-commerce vs. e-business in the late 1990s – how did we ever waste so much time on this? The distinction between content and process is an important one however. Business coaches need to be able to explain how they achieve change through their particular brand of coaching. They need to be able to demonstrate a process that has validity to a buyer. They do not all have, of course, to agree on what that process is. Although the process itself may not be immediately visible to the naked eye of the one being coached, it underlies and guides the coach's decisions about what to cover in order to facilitate the desired changes.

In some cases, coaches will need to be quite explicit about how or why their chosen process creates results or what the underpinning science is. One of our US banking clients once asked us for a full dissertation about the theoretical under-pinning of our work: scary, sobering and ultimately fascinating . . .

So business coaches need to choose a framework – be it a sports metaphor or a clever acronym – and then be prepared to use it flexibly while justifying it clearly. This is what we do in the next chapter.

3

The practice of business coaching

This chapter presents the practitioner's view. What works and why it works: both a model for best practice and a demonstration of which psychological 'technologies' we use in our everyday work.

For the buyer of coaching, it will provide an overall review of what to look for when identifying competent coaches (a disarming question is to ask a coach what he or she actually plans to *do* with the client). For the aspiring coach who has not spent six years at university studying psychology, it will provide a robust background to both the human condition and the psychological processes fundamental to achieving lasting change. Business coaches from a non-psychological background should enjoy this selection of the more obviously useful concepts, and be guided towards further reading. Finally, clients should find it amusing to discover explicitly some of the mechanisms which make them behave in a certain way, and use this knowledge to refine their people management skills.

When we start working with a new client, we use a roughly-sketched map. Independently of which framework business coaches choose they use an overall approach for the coaching relationship. A useful analogy is that a coaching engagement is a business programme, with each session set up as a short project. Like all programmes, it has review points, various stakeholders and built-in flexibility. Like all programmes the projects are interdependent and can be run to some degree in parallel. Finally, it also has clear deliverables and a post-engagement review.

Our coaching programmes follow the five components of our business coaching framework:

- Build the relationship
- Draw out the picture
- Achieve change
- Motivate for results
- Conclude the relationship

This is not a linear framework: it has clear entry and exit points but is a highly recurrent process between them as expressed in Figure 3.1.

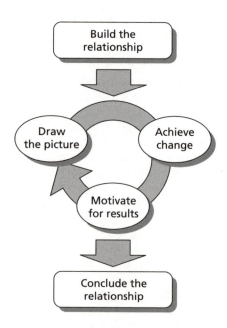

Figure 3.1 **The business coaching framework.**

Build the relationship

The real process of business coaching begins with the establishment of a trusting relationship with the client. The business coach will need to earn the client's trust in at least three areas: professional competence, understanding and confidentiality. Critical to these are first the attitude of the coach and then their professional skill.

When the ancient Greeks sought enlightenment of the Delphic Oracle, the text above the portal exhorted 'Know thyself'. This is fundamental advice for all coaches. Insight and self-awareness are essential prerequisites to development for clients. It is where all coaching has to start. Insight into their own attitudes, judgements and possible blind spots is also a vital prerequisite for business coaches to be highly effective. Skills can be learned fairly easily and practised into behaviour patterns. Attitudes need more work. Coaches from a business background in particular tend to have a harder time switching off 'experience', that is, impatient judgement, pre-packaged solutions and the burning desire to act as experts.

A client recently described a senior manager who had made an in-depth study of interpersonal communication theory. His learning was solidly intellectual. He could discuss topics such as motivation, personality and character strengths in detail. He had tremendous insight into the psychological make-up of his colleagues. However, despite his good intentions, he was described by several of his colleagues as 'painting by numbers'. Each colour was carefully and correctly applied in a meticulous fashion but the end result was never art. What seemed to be lacking was a sense of his underlying respect for and warmth towards people. His actions were perceived as sterile and in-authentic – even manipulative – when they were, in fact, well intentioned. Attitudes pervade our speech, our tone of voice, the vocabulary we use and all our body language. Words we can choose carefully or even fake, but attitudes can easily leak out non-verbally. There are some attitudes that seem vital to the coaching process.

The work of Carl Rogers in the 1950s in analysing the characteristics of the helping relationship is a historically relevant, if surprising, place to start in examining the nature of the coaching relationship. 'Helping' may sound like a strangely soft term but he defined it as where one party has 'the intent of promoting the growth, development, maturity, improved functioning or improved coping with life of the other'. Empirical research in the field of attitudes had shown that in parent-child relationships, the so-called 'acceptant-democratic' seemed the most facilitative style for development. Whatever the type of helper – parent, doctor, therapist or nowadays coach – the key elements in the relationship seemed to be establishing trust, giving independence and ensuring the other felt understood. Direct specific advice came out as unhelpful. Yet more than 50 years later many business relationships are still based on being rather judgemental and 'giving people the benefit of your experience' – however ineffective both prove to be. Expert communicators in a range of fields use very different techniques from the novice. The desire and the ability to understand and accept your client's meanings and feelings, sensitivity to a client's attitudes and warm interest without over-involvement all mark out the more professional business coach.

The coaching relationship can be a very delicate and powerful one. In studies using galvanic skin response (GSR), which measures fine variations in anxiety, even a slight lessening of the degree of acceptance by the listener led to GSR deviations. This indicates a sense of threat in the client detected at a physiological level. Therefore, the perceived attitudes and feelings of the coach have a huge impact on the nature of the relationship. They may, in fact, be more relevant to success than the specific orientation, procedures and techniques used by the coach. The most critical factors determining the efficacy of the coaching relationship are empathy, positive attitude and respect.

Empathy

Empathy indicates an understanding and acceptance of someone else's emotional situation. The coach's words must match the internal feelings and the intensity of their affective expression must be congruent with the client's. This requires close observation and matching of both the nature and strength of emotion, expressed in conjunction with careful listening to the perceived facts. If a client is, for instance, describing their frustration, it is the coach's critical role to understand and help calibrate the nature and degree of the emotion rather than moving quickly into action to change the situation. Empathy – the capacity to see and feel as the other does without evaluation or judgement – is a critical starting point in establishing and maintaining rapport. If coaches are unaware of their own feelings then communication may contain contradictions of a subtle and non-verbal nature. Most people do use empathy to some limited degree in their natural communication but failure to exercise it fully in coaching will limit the process to a fairly superficial level of interaction.

When brainstorming with heads of government departments in the Cayman Islands about the underlying attitudes in coaching, one of the perhaps surprising attitudes they proposed was 'loving them to bits'. Interestingly, this suggestion emanated from the prison governor and the chief of police!

Positive attitude

This may need a careful definition. It is defined as a component of happiness and measured by the PANAS test (Watson *et al*. 1988). It also measures the degree of positive attitude of a coach. A positive attitude involves warmth, caring, liking, interest and respect. In practical terms, it means being absolutely there for the other person. Being on their side does not lead to a loss of objectivity. It is only once this acceptance has been established that a coach can encourage someone to test the accuracy of their own perceptions and try on alternative interpretations and actions. In business settings, people are often either unfamiliar with these emotions or quite afraid of them. They hide behind 'professional' or impersonal, even quite cold, relationships. The business coach has the opportunity to demonstrate a straightforward positive attitude and be accepting enough to cope with the emotions the client will experience. A business coach's positive attitude will often spring from an open-ended belief in the astonishing capacity of people to change and develop. Limiting self-beliefs can harm coaches as well as their clients.

Respect

A respectful attitude may seem easy, but can be quite hard in some situations. This usually indicates an underlying belief held by the coach which makes for a negative judgement. The Danish philosopher Kierkegaard said, 'If you would change a tyrant first start where the tyrant is'. Which takes us back to empathy again. Business coaches will deal with a very wide range of often quite driven people. Their success may have come about through the use of both techniques and communication styles at odds with a good business coach's preferred style. In the early days of coaching we would often invite companies to give us their most difficult people to coach. These people had often achieved high status roles, and nicknames such as 'Attila the Hun' or 'The Anti-Christ'. Their style was often aggressive and at times downright offensive. Partway through the first coaching session, it was extraordinary to realise that those labels were forgotten as we found out how fantastic they were as people. Usually highly motivated, they were not difficult people. They just had really difficult ways. Colleagues often never see beyond that. Finding even just the one thing you respect in any individual switches perception of them and makes coaching possible. This functions much as visual perception illusions do. The first image we see in such a puzzle often locks out our capacity to see anything else. Actively recognising our attitude blocks and taking steps to shift them is vital in business coaching where we can rarely choose the style of client we will work with. Façades and political games may encourage role-playing, sycophancy and some deception in organisations. The respectful coach may be the only person who can hold up a mirror to clients with honesty. Keeping free from external judgement, on occasions even the positive, allows the recognition that the locus of evaluation is internal, situated in the clients themselves. It is not the coach's role to approve or disapprove but rather to invoke the client's own balanced judgement. Coaching aims to keep putting control back in the clients' hands. How rationally they judge their own achievements is important to sustaining lasting changes made through coaching.

Rogers, in 1958, described human relationships as 'The most critical enterprise in today's world . . .'. He argued that 'it is not upon the physical sciences that the future will depend. It is upon us who are trying to understand and deal with the interactions between human beings'. A responsible and professional attitude to the process of coaching is a prerequisite for being a successful business coach. Failure to observe even higher standards of businesslike professionalism than are attained in the client's business setting will and should earn a coach a bad reputation. However, while assiduous attention to the outward signs of trustworthiness is vital, such as appointments that are kept punctually, confidentiality that is upheld, commitments that are followed through, rigid consistency is not in fact the key to successful business coaching. Unambiguous, respectful and warm communication is.

Soft is hard . . .

People have fallen into the habit of describing the science of human relations in organisations as the 'soft' skills. In fact they turn out to be very hard skills judging by how little they are used in effective ways in organisations. These sophisticated interpersonal skills may be natural in some people but for most they have to be learned and improved upon to achieve highly effective results.

In many organisations, pains will be taken to establish rapport before the coaching assignment is agreed. Introductions will be made to several coaches and the clients will choose the business coach they wish to work with. Although people may start off with a list of professional requirements, the decision will often be taken on the basis of chemistry and rapport. First impressions are powerful and good coaches do themselves few favours by not ensuring that they take this part of the process very seriously. The qualities that make them good coaches should guarantee that they are sensitive and aware of the needs of the client, but sometimes this part of the process is overlooked. They may automatically launch into coaching when that is not what the client wants at that stage. Building rapport requires basic good manners and 'meet and greet' sensitivity. Impressions are often formed in the first 30 seconds of encounter and take a much longer time to correct if inaccurate. Body posture, eye contact and level of attention are among the non-verbal cues that contribute to rapport. Probably of most significance is demonstration of interest in the other person with specific concern and sensitivity regarding their feelings about being in this current, and possibly alien, situation. This is not a stage at which a coach should be attempting to impress with deep and meaningful insights. However, there often is a need to establish credentials in some way that shows capabilities in action. This might take the form of describing comparable assignments or more wide ranging business involvement. Storytelling is a valuable process throughout the various stages of coaching.

Agreement about the nature and scope of confidentiality is an important foundation for relationship-building. Clients take their own time to assess how truly you embody the concept of confidentiality and some may test you by gradually revealing information and checking how you handle it. Even where clients do not seem concerned about who knows what, it is very important that the coach takes the responsibility for debating and agreeing the bounds of confidentiality in each contract. Decisions are made at this stage about how feedback on progress is given to the company or sponsoring individual and how much is revealed in the coach's own supervision relationship. Confidentiality is addressed more fully in Chapter 7.

Draw the picture

Raise awareness

Most clients benefit from the opportunity to take stock of their situation as objectively as possible. Some may be unrealistically self-critical, while others may be blithely unaware of the impact of their actions. In either case, receiving feedback from people in the organisation or through psychometric assessment is an excellent way of enabling clear and constructive self-awareness. Many organisations have their own sophisticated 360° assessment process which can be used as a starting point in coaching. Often, although the information has been given, the acceptance, understanding and agreement as to the requisite action required to change the picture have not been fully explored with the client within the organisational setting.

At its simplest, sending an e-mail to an agreed list of colleagues and bosses along the lines of 'list the three things you would want X to start doing, stop doing or continue doing' can get right to the heart of the matter and give much needed and desired feedback. It is often best to ensure confidentiality by collating the feedback as it is only human to try to work out who said what. If respondents know themselves to be protected by confidentiality, they will be more honest than if they run the risk of having their irate boss demanding why they said what they did. Probably something about their boss's aggressive nature in that last case we would imagine!

Psychometric assessment is also invaluable – not as a 'tablet of stone', irrefutable truth but rather as a starting point for discussion which enables you to leave no stone unturned in exploring the individual's preferred style. Tests are often used, abused and misunderstood, reducing people to a mere collection of letters or graphs. This is a misuse of the instruments and against the original purpose of the testing. In this day and age, flexibility and innovation are essential. By allowing clients to narrowly define and hence limit themselves, we would be losing the opportunity to help them recognise the strengths which they can bring to bear to learn to behave and perform differently in a whole range of new situations.

Many of these measures need correct training in administration and interpretation. It is worth experimenting to find the ones which are, on the one hand well established and verified, but which also have the best validity for the style of coaching you wish to do. Experienced coaches have often spent a lifetime collecting questionnaires and exercises which they find especially useful both at the commencement of coaching and throughout the process.

Observe

Whenever opportunities present themselves it can be very enlightening to have the opportunity to observe the client functioning in the real world – giving a presentation, leading a meeting or even in conversation. This gives an opportunity to check their perception of themselves against reality. One of our colleagues who specialises in sales coaching actually accompanies his clients on calls as a 'helper'. Otherwise, observing within the coaching session is critical. How clients relate to and deal with the coach gives clues about their relationships with others which can be fed back and adjusted for effectiveness.

Legitimise

Clients sometimes describe coaching as the opportunity for a sanity check. In organisations where weaknesses or doubts are not expressed openly, the coaching relationship is perhaps the one place where reservations can be tested. It is often important for clients to have their feelings legitimised (e.g. 'many people might feel the way you do in these circumstances' or 'anyone would find it difficult to step into this new role'). Respect was mentioned as an attitude essential to the coaching relationship, and clear statements of respect are important during coaching sessions: 'I am impressed by how you handled that'.

Explore

The most deceptively simple skill used in business coaching is that of listening. People take it for granted that we all possess that skill and as a result may overlook the need to hone it to a higher level of efficacy. Speech is described by psychologists as 'telegraphic'. We do not need to hear entire conversations to gain an understanding of the message being imparted. In overheard conversation, we can often put two and two together, admittedly to make 35 on some occasions. Our minds fill in the gaps. This is common in conversation where people, having heard enough, often start to plan their response before the other speaker finishes. They may then go on to worry about how to respond if the other person doesn't like their comment and how to deal with that, and on and on. All before the speaker has finished. They are missing out on vital components of information. This is often how we listen in normal social circumstances without even realising. In effective coaching, listening quality is of a very different order. It is often described as active listening, empathic listening or listening on all cylinders. When coaching managers in using a coaching style of communication, it can take a whole day to break the pattern of leaping in with advice rather than even listening to the end of the story. Excellent coaches are listening for what is being said, what is being omitted, the way in which it is being said, the other illustrative body language that might change the meaning of the words, all while following the links to previous themes. The client basks in the full beam of the coach's attention. It is, however, still not enough to just carry out this amazing feat. A two-dimensional cardboard cut-out with a tape recorder would be just as good to talk to otherwise. It is essential also to communicate the fact that this focused listening is happening, while not taking the spotlight away from the client. Often this is done through small facilitative gestures – nodding, 'uh huhs' or facial expression. It is one of the few times when leading questions are allowable and productive such as 'And then?' or by repeating something just said but in a questioning tone. This guides the client on without breaking their flow of concentration and thought processes.

Questions are an essential way of exploring issues. Most business people could tell you about open and closed questions in their sleep. There are advanced techniques for questioning, such as those derived from David Grove's work on clean language (Lawley and Tompkins 2000). Yet there seems to be little impact on everyday communication style. It is easy for people to slip into heavily constructed, thinking aloud, multiple and confusing questions. When observing trainee coaches, what you often find is a tendency to attempt to craft really fabulously constructed open questions. By contrast, the old hand will drop their voice and say, 'And, now?' to astonishing effect. Another challenge for the coach is always to check why you asked a particular question. Often we can ask for information that is spurious and removes focus from the key issues. As Sir William Mosler said, 'If all you ever ask is questions, all you ever get is answers'. Communication in business coaching is much more varied and subtle than a stream of Q&A.

Research into communication by general practitioners has shown that what they ask in the first few minutes of a conversation can determine whether they will ever get to the bottom of an issue. Evidence indicated that it is easy to close off an avenue of discussion by too eagerly leaping ahead with ill-judged questions. This is referred to as 'premature closure' – jumping to conclusions about issues and pursuing them rather than keeping the discussion wide at an early stage.

Questions have a powerful role in exploring the issues when they make the other person stop and reconsider their perception of an event or a reaction rather than blandly accepting the rationale they habitually take. The word 'why' sometimes gets a bad press in communication literature as it is seen as being too aggressive. However, when contemplatively and respectfully or even humorously asked, it can challenge blind assumptions and unnoticed belief systems that have limited someone's functioning for years. A very successful client who was looking at the next stage in his career was asked what he would choose to do in an ideal world. 'Learn to windsurf when I retire,' he replied. The next question, 'Why not now?' was met with a horrified look, silence and some emotion. He realised in that moment that he was not letting himself do the things he enjoyed because of guilt about his father having to work hard all his life for a much poorer standard of living than this man now had. He challenged his own assumptions, weighed up the facts and decided that he could afford to take three whole weeks to master this new skill without damaging his career or his deeply-held values. Re-energised by his sporting achievements over the summer he went on to scale new business heights.

In business coaching, probing questions are productive. Once trust is well established business clients can find the personal challenge which comes from clear insight into their behaviour very valuable. It is distinct from the point-scoring challenge of some colleagues and gives them the opportunity to raise their game considerably. With high achievement and status, such people are often accorded unquestioning respect in their organisation, at least overtly. Only the business coach may have the privileged relationship that will allow for this type of challenge.

Questions are vital for helping the client clarify thinking which may have become muddled and convoluted. Teasing out the logic from supposition, the fact from fantasy, allows the individual to embark on problem-solving much more readily.

Finally, it is always worth exploring the notion of secondary gain when questioning clients. Classic secondary gain in psychology is often about sickness behaviour and the unconscious appreciation of being looked after. In business, there are also many examples such as holding back ambition while retaining the support of peers. Good business coaches will use a combination of techniques to probe and challenge the evidence presented. Linguistic techniques such as the metamodel (Bandler and Grinder 1975) which replace the traditional 'Why?' with 'For what purpose?' can be very effective when trying to find the answer beyond the obvious cognitive one.

Achieve change

Once the various elements of the picture have become clear, a number of things will happen. Some issues will disappear by simple virtue of having being made explicit or being reframed, as in the surfing example above. There is also a danger that, having identified an issue, the client treats it as something already addressed. It is therefore important at this stage that the client makes the change (as opposed to the goal) explicit. The coach must also be very careful to pass the responsibility for change to the client. In other words, the coach must 'disown' the change.

Negotiate carefully defined goals

Care at this stage will determine the success of the coaching. The purposes of coaching may include some of the following:

- Transition from one role or state to another
- Dealing with change
- Resolution of issues
- Skill development
- Achieving excellence

What is critical is that the client owns the process and determines the goals rather than them being imposed or assumed by the coach. This is important for a number of reasons. It exemplifies the nature of the relationship. Coaching is always defined as a partnership. In transaction analysis terms, it means that all transactions should be 'adult to adult'. Due to the strength of the relationship, coaches have the opportunity to wield a very powerful influence over their clients, who may seek approval and therefore do what the coach seems to want rather than test options and make their own informed choices. It is vital to avoid forming an unproductive dependency in a client who cannot make a decision without consulting their coach first. Think of Eddie in *Absolutely Fabulous* for a parody of the situation where someone stops thinking and deciding for themselves because they have a coach to do it instead and take the blame if it goes wrong. Another basic reason for having the client take the decision is just that it works better. Human beings resist all change that is imposed on them. Where we initiate change ourselves there is a far higher likelihood that we will see it through to its final conclusion. Where there is affirmation, ownership of a decision or a commitment, such as 'I have decided to work on these aspects of leadership', there is a higher likelihood of follow-through and achievement than will follow, 'You should think about working on these aspects of leadership'. Such is human nature.

A key distinction between business coaching and life coaching is that, in the former, goals need to be useful and realistic for all three parties involved in the transaction. We have had cases for example where the client was ready to change the world by entering a new market or heading-up a new division, totally unaware that the current perception of the client by his organisation was that he was not up to it. Obviously such surprises should be managed up front and mitigated both by negotiating objectives for the coaching programme and collecting objective feedback on the client. Business coaching however is different in the sense that objectives may include more stages such as demonstrating new capabilities or putting in place a tailored communication plan in advance of launching into new business activities.

This situation was quite frequent when people either sought their own coaching, perhaps with the company just picking up the bill, or were given coaching contacts and allowed to get on with it with the assumption that benefits would come back to the organisation eventually. Today, more and more companies are looking to involve the business coach by keeping them aware of the talent management processes that are being adopted and by linking the coach and the company sponsor in a team supporting the individual in achievement of goals. Coaches need to be particularly skilled as consultants, drawing out issues and assessing and communicating the goals that the organisation requires their employee to achieve. This preparation is somewhat easier when the decision to offer coaching is the result of an appraisal, in the formation of personal development plans or because of a change in role or responsibilities.

People do not regularly or voluntarily update their views of others. Fundamentally, underneath it all, they may have a suspicion that people do not really change. They often cling to their stereotyped views despite much evidence to the contrary. Once they have pigeonholed someone, they may not notice the many subtle changes that have taken place as part of the development through coaching. It can be very important to have the company sponsor or the line manager actively looking for discernible changes. This provides ongoing feedback, support and challenge for the client. The contract is therefore rarely only with the client and the coach. At the very least it includes the organisation as a whole. The trick is in compartmentalising communication in such a way that agreed themes may be fed back, with the permission of the client, while the integrity of confidentiality is upheld.

Another subtle task for a business coach is to manage the portfolio of goals for the coaching programme with objectivity and flexibility. Coaching is often described as very client led: people often present with one set of objectives which can be thrown into disarray when they start to explore the issue. Also, companies tend to brief coaches along a narrow set of business agenda items, whereas clients are likely to want to fit them, however indirectly, around other issues such as family and health, for example. While the coach is, in a sense, entirely on their client's side they must check how appropriate it is to move fully onto the other's agenda without challenging the value and appropriateness. Companies will want to see the results they contracted for and it is important to keep this in mind while also taking into account the client's broader agenda.

Once agreed, goals need to be clearly defined. Most people are familiar with the concept of SMART goals: specific, measurable, achievable, realistic and time-bound. Nonetheless, they still tend to state their goals vaguely, such as a desire to 'be a better manager', 'become an effective leader' or worse still in terms of what they do not want. Careful analysis and refining of goals gives them a better chance of being achieved and the opportunity for positive reinforcement at stages along the way. Gradual approximation to desired goals by breaking tasks down into smaller, achievable and rewarded steps is more likely to guarantee success. Sometimes a bit of lateral thinking is required but we like to use the approach of a US technology company which we know well: 'absolutely everybody gets measured, no matter how subjective their job. For example our "evangelists" are measured not in terms of sales they generate; that would be too vague and too distant. We track the number of face-to-face meetings with board level clients each month instead'.

Sometimes the most successful people still feel like failures because they do not recognise the achievement of goals along the way. Reminding them that the only way to eat an elephant is 'in small mouthfuls' is often salutary.

The behavioural tradition of quantified goals and measured outcomes is equally attractive to the coaching relationship and to the organisation.

Giving feedback

Feedback is often badly handled in organisations because much as people know intellectually that they should give it, they rarely do to the degree that benefits most people. It is often unbalanced. There is a strong negative bias despite the rise of books such as *The One Minute Manager* (Blanchard and Johnson 2004) which preach concepts like 'catch people doing something right and tell them'. Many people learn that the offer of 'just a little feedback' is likely to be an unpleasant business. Even where there is a regular in-house appraisal system, this may not take into account the quality of the communication skills of the appraiser. Appraisal systems have sometimes been referred to as 'exercises in ritual humiliation' by their recipients. Insufficient recognition is given for results. Feedback is often given in a way which does not immediately link to the relevant changes which would lead to success. It can have a 'pull your socks up' tone to it without defining which socks and how far.

Having been through an experience like that, even only once, is likely to make people question the value and avoid seeking out feedback in the future.

There is also a clear bias in people themselves for perceiving what has not been done or completed, more strongly than they acknowledge their successes. This is known as the Zeigarnik effect. It may be that we are hard-wired to behave like this, as it can be a useful survival mechanism, stopping us from resting on our laurels for any length of time. However, it has been shown to make people destructively pessimistic and often quite blind to the strengths they use on a daily basis. Coaching people to give themselves feedback on their own achievements gives them an opportunity to recognise which strengths they have used and how they can apply them in other, newer situations. Research from positive psychology also shows that it is also likely to raise their levels of life satisfaction.

A client was becoming increasingly dissatisfied with his role in a private equity investment organisation despite evident success. He worked exceedingly long hours, appointments were constantly being changed and he often could not see any worthwhile achievement. He was contemplating leaving his excellent job. The simple expedient of noting the three things that had gone well each day and analysing his own contribution to them had a dramatic effect. After a fortnight his perception, and consequently his satisfaction levels, were radically altered, leaving him clear-thinking about how he could contribute most constructively to his company, through career development and focus, that made the most of his strengths.

The business coach has a unique opportunity for the type of feedback that can be rare in an organisational setting. 'Here and now' immediacy is specific to the way the client is thinking, behaving or speaking and can be utilised in the session. For example, if a client dismisses an idea in an aggressive way, the coach can use self-disclosure to feed back the emotional impact. As it is given for pure purposes with no personal axe to grind, it can be seen as more unbiased and acceptable. This goes for the positive perhaps especially, which is not dismissed by the client as empty flattery, thus making it much more effective.

'Here and now' refers to observations during the coaching session. It might be about incongruence in speech and body language (e.g. where someone is talking about being excited about a new initiative, but is doing so in a monotone). Feedback in real time gives the individual the time to consider whether this is because they do not actually feel positive or because they have no understanding of the impact of non-verbal communication on the overall message. Coaching can then pick out the themes and proceed appropriately. Business coaches, unlike colleagues, do not always take everything at face value.

Video feedback is a useful asset here in both bringing immediate self-awareness and in enabling clients to see for themselves the advances they have made by adopting changes in their performance. Video is often a reflection of the client's self-perception: initially they find only weaknesses but through objective dialogue rapidly realise that they are much better than they initially thought!

Reinforcement

Feedback is one of the basic forms of reinforcement derived from behavioural psychology. Pavlov and his dog have passed into popular culture. Of most importance is the fact that behavioural approaches are always experimental. Observations and baseline assessments are made. Goals are established. Techniques are employed to alter the outcomes. Results are measured and adjustments are made to approximate closer to the achievement of goals. Coaching works best when it is based on this process. This is not however to argue that the reinforcing should lie solely in the hands of the coach. Links with sponsors in the company are also useful here.

The rigorous measurement of contingencies and reinforcement are extremely important in assessing performance in modern organisations. Without attention to these, change will decay quickly and individuals and cultures revert to type. Reward is generally recognised as having major importance in achieving and maintaining changes in behaviour. However, lack of understanding of the complexities of reinforcement often prevents its most effective use.

Response-contingent positive reinforcement may be easy for psychologists to say but is a closed book to many managers and perhaps some coaches. Coaching a client to recognise and use different types and patterns of reinforcement makes them more effective in their corporate role. These techniques are often cheap and more effective than some of the complex reward systems set up in organisations. Even the basic primary re-inforcement of recognition through greetings and thank-yous is surprisingly overlooked, yet will often be the first criticism picked up in a culture audit. Coaches, leading by example, demonstrate the efficacy of timely, focused reinforcement.

Rehearsal

Rehearsal can be effectively used in coaching. Clients will often have achieved a great deal of intellectual learning about concepts such as communication and leadership. They may, as a result, have acquired insight into their own inadequacies or bad habits in the area. This alone will not change their performance. In fact, over-intellectualising can on occasion slow down progress. Perfectionists may want to know everything about a topic before embarking on risky exposure. In behavioural psychology, the concept of synchronicity refers to this alignment of mind, body and behaviour. At various stages in development one of the modalities may be established while the others are dragging behind. For instance, in public speaking, one client may know exactly how to do it, may feel more positive as a result of coaching but somehow never makes the opportunity. Another may also have the knowledge, speaks regularly but has not yet overcome the anticipatory anxiety. The popular saying 'Fake it 'til you make it' has value. It is only when clients try out new learning in action that they can improve the alignment of their knowledge, feeling and behaviours. Testing out new behaviours during the coaching session, the client can then explore what feelings may emerge and which aspects of behaviour and new skills they need to work on. For instance, just reading about these skills here will not make you into a professional coach. It is only through practice, refining through feedback and reward, that you will develop the required skills. Coaching entails locking that knowledge into observable and productive actions back in the day job. So if we want people to know, feel and do better then practice within sessions is essential.

In some cases, clients have a long-held belief about themselves that they think may require some form of psychotherapy. The competent business coach will first probe and challenge and then decide on the limits of their intervention (this is covered in great detail in Chapter 7). They will also reframe the belief by checking for evidence in the present rather than the past. Finally, rehearsal can be a remarkable tool to overcome unresolved issues: if you can fake it long enough, you may well end up believing it . . .

Modelling

There are two techniques which are both referred to as modelling. One refers to acting as a model for the other, showing how it is or can be done. The second version involves modelling as you would clay, building up in the other person the final performance they require.

In making new knowledge very practical it can be important for the coach to demonstrate how it can be done. In a sense, working with managers the coach is all the time demonstrating a better way of getting results with people which by itself has an impact on the client. In other, more specific, settings seeing how the coach might handle a situation or deal with a difficulty is giving a role model for change. Models of perfection are however best avoided. We have all probably experienced the situation when watching someone really good just makes us feel, 'I will never be able to do that'. It is only when the performance is then broken down into its component parts that the client can begin to benefit from a demonstration. A tennis coach showing a perfect serve may inspire but will not necessarily improve the other's technique. It is only when the service is broken down into several specific moves and each is practised separately that muscle memory is formed and the learning occurs at a personal level. Often rather than demonstrating an expert version, especially where communication is involved, a coach achieves better results through shaping up the other's performance. Again using the public speaking example, using practice where clients critique themselves and by gradual approximations achieve their eventual goal.

There is ample literature about modelling approaches. Coaches may turn to Dilts's work at FIAT (1998) or to Tim Gallwey's first tome on sports modelling (1974).

Challenging ineffective thinking

In business coaching, clients are bright and often very aware of what they should be doing. What holds them back is more likely to be a set of limiting beliefs.

The richness of cognitive approaches developed through the research of Albert Ellis (Ellis and Grieger 1977) and Aaron Beck (1976) offers so much for the coach to use to enhance the confidence, emotions and resultant performance of their clients. People are often unaware of the underlying beliefs and assumptions that they have. They have been formed by previous experiences or associations. When confronting a new situation, automatic thoughts will determine the emotional reaction and in turn the behaviour of the individual, often without their being aware of the process. As a result, performance is impacted on or situations avoided altogether. Common thinking errors are:

- Using wrong labels
- All or nothing thinking
- Over-generalising
- Exaggerating or catastrophising
- Ignoring the positive
- Negatively predicting the future

Coaches can help clients become aware of their thought processes (what went through your mind right there?), make explicit any thinking errors or cognitive distortions and demonstrate the impact these negative expectancies have on emotions and behaviour. They can then coach clients to dispute the evidence for and against, recognising the emotion evoked by the thoughts, and to assess the impact on the actual and desired behavioural outcome. This can enable clients to continue to develop good techniques and resultant well-being and success. The recognition of particular, recurring styles of thinking error

Table 3.1 Learned optimism

	Confident attitude		Not confident	
	Success	*Failure*	*Success*	*Failure*
Permanent	Good things always happen to me	It was just on this occasion that it failed	It was a fluke	Bad things always happen to me
Pervasive	Everything goes well for me	It was just this one thing that went wrong	It was just this one thing that went right	Everything always goes wrong
Personal	I worked hard for that	It was a bad interview	Anyone could have done that	I'm not good enough

points at underlying beliefs. By addressing and assessing these, coaches will often enable the client to release more energy in a positive and purposeful way through new, more optimistic beliefs.

The work by Martin Seligman on learned optimism and defensive pessimism (1991) is useful in coaching. By analysing whether thinking is permanent, pervasive and personal for success and failure and reviewing the research evidence on success and well-being in optimists, the coach has good grounds for helping clients change their thinking styles to achieve more constructive success (see Table 3.1).

Motivating for results

There are many areas in our lives where we know exactly what we should be doing, yet somehow we just don't do the things that we know to be right. Health is an easy example. Most people have a good idea about how they should eat, drink and exercise. That alone does not make it happen. Yet sometimes it is as if a switch has been flicked and we are suddenly ready to translate the knowledge we have into action. It does not even seem like an effort any more. If that kind of motivation could be bottled, it would be so easy for everyone to make the necessary changes at the right time. As it is, we need to look at what are the likely variables that might cause the tipping point for change as efficiently as possible.

Stages of change

Prochaska's stages of change (Prochaska and DiClemente 1982) is a useful tool in determining someone's preparedness for change and in choosing appropriate coaching initiatives. The stages are as follows.

Pre-contemplation, or 'what problem?'

At this stage it would be very difficult to motivate someone to action. They may not see the need to change or believe in the possibility of change. This is where awareness-raising is most important. Appraisal and formulations of personal development plans may allow the person to recognise opportunities for change. It is very important at this stage for coaches not to be carried away by their own enthusiasm. This will lead to resistance and even rejection of the process out of hand. Extra time may have to be spent reviewing the data and finding ways of testing out reality so that the client can begin to see why they might want to be coached.

Contemplation, or 'not quite ready'

At this stage the person has become more aware of options. For example they may have heard about coaching and may be seeking information. Discussions with colleagues who have been coached or consultations with HR are useful. The coach may have to help the client try on a different reality or review 'what ifs' while working on building a trustworthy relationship.

Preparation, decision, determination, or 'I will soon'

This often occurs in the early stages of coaching when the individual is weighing up options, considering how and when to make a difference and formulating plans. The coach's role might involve encouraging clients to undertake a cost/benefit analysis of the options, to keep a log of behaviours and to plan objectives carefully.

Taking action, or real behaviour change

At this stage the client is ready to implement action plans, test out new options and observe the benefits of the change. Problem-solving, support and reinforcement are the most valuable coaching skills at this stage.

Maintenance, or hanging on to the change

In order to lock-in a changed set of behaviours and intentions, practice and over-learning are usually necessary. Old habits have to decay while new ones are established. The results have to be deemed sufficiently rewarding to deserve the effort it might take to incorporate them into the new repertoire. This often requires troubleshooting and review of any lapses and their impact. The coach needs to establish a pattern of self-reinforcement in clients to ensure behaviour and attitude change is maintained.

Relapse, or 'uh-oh . . .'

Old habits die hard and it is likely that at some stage clients will revert to old styles of behaviour. Support and encouragement, legitimisation – 'this happens to most people making major changes' – and help in reformulating goals and action plans are most appropriate. It is often important to plan for this eventuality in a constructive way before it happens.

People have to move from one stage to the next during a process of change. Pacing is an important coaching skill. Very experienced coaches may rarely make it explicit but they are constantly noticing the signs that guide them as to whether to challenge someone to move on or to let them go more slowly at each stage. This is fundamental to long-term and lasting success. Empathy and close observation are critical in staying in tune with the client and harnessing their motivation. Rushing them can often slow down or disrupt the process in the long run.

Personal drivers

Understanding what drives a particular person can help make the changes relevant. Few people are solely motivated by monetary reward. For some it can be the opportunity to exercise power and influence or for others the chance to use their expertise or to gain status. Unless coaches and their clients understand the nature of motivation they cannot harness it fully. By discovering what has driven them in the past, it is easy to adapt that to current situations. For example, as discussed in Chapter 4, many people nowadays are required to sell as part of their role. It works best if they can understand how to motivate themselves – rather than 'I have to sell to ten people' the more expertise-focused individual can state the alternative, 'I can give ten people the benefit of my insight into this product'. This should put them in a more positive state of mind to go out there and get on with it.

A way to look at personal drivers is to identify and utilise the values of the client concerning a certain subject. Some are context independent (e.g. 'it is important to compete') but many are very specific to a particular work or life area. Some coaches ask the question directly (i.e. 'What is important to you in your career?') while others will want to use a measurement from a pre-established list such as signature strengths (Peterson and Seligman 2004).

Bringing the relationship to a conclusion

Coaching depends on an intense, empathic and professional relationship. If successful, by the end, the client should feel equipped and ready to continue without the coaching support. It can be very tempting for a coach to extend this time if only to find out the end of their client's story. Coaching will, however, have failed in a major respect if the client remains dependent after the last session. Assessing whether the work is done or whether there is a need or purpose to extend the coaching is an essential professional skill. A purchaser of coaching recently said he had never yet encountered a coach just trying to make more money out of a client. However, it may be that there are times when people are motivated to keep the relationship going for other reasons.

Perhaps the psychodynamic approach should not be overlooked – even by dyed in the wool cognitive behaviourists who clamour for methodologically sound, research-based evidence. Theories on transference and countertransference are invaluable in monitoring the nature of the relationship between coach and client. Combined with clear and strongly adhered-to professional ethics this can ensure that clients are correctly dealt with and that coaching terminates at an appropriate stage. Transference in therapy describes the process by which the therapist becomes someone significant to the other (e.g. parent, lover, friend). Countertransference is when the patient similarly takes on particular significance to the therapist. In therapy, this is seen as inevitable and giving important leverage at certain stages of treatment. There are some parallels in coaching. The relationship is an intense one, with mutual respect and a great deal of trust. It is carried out behind closed doors with an intimacy and an openness which is perhaps not repeated elsewhere in the client's life. The approval of the coach may be unlike anything the client receives from their boss or even their marital partner. Experienced coaches who achieve great results are usually aware of the powerful nature of the relationship and are careful how they wield it as a result. By the time the end of the sessions is reached the process of separation is well in place. Naïve coaches can be caught out and taken aback if, for instance, a sense of attraction or attachment occurs during the coaching. Again, 'know thyself' is a critical maxim. The unaware coach can end up blurring boundaries in ways which may not be professional.

Those with therapeutic backgrounds are used to utterly black and white ethical guidelines set up to protect both parties from abuse of a situation. This extends to socialising, accepting gifts and soliciting business. Coaches who have come from other disciplines may be less used to these stringent standards. Without an understanding of these concepts, coaches can be taken unawares by their own feelings or those of their clients and may not make the best use of these opportunities when they occur. Some of these issues are discussed in Chapter 7.

Sometimes simple actions such as extending the time between final sessions can begin the process of separation and reduction of dependency.

Closure in business coaching will also encompass a detailed review of original objectives, clear recognition of results and the original decisions made about feedback to the commissioning organisation and sponsors. The client should be fully involved in deciding whether additional themes should be fed back and how this should be done for the best results.

In conclusion

Techniques such as those described in this chapter will enhance the repertoire of the coach but will be of little value if not rooted in an excellent relationship between coach and client. The person-centred approach and the work of Carl Rogers have essential lessons for coaching. Coaches, like therapists, are more effective when they demonstrate the fundamental relationship skills of genuineness, positive regard and empathy. For many coaching clients in business there may be few other relationships where these conditions occur. Empathy allows an understanding of their subjective reality – reflecting back a recognition of some of the emotions and thoughts which are not spoken anywhere else. The skills of restatement, paraphrasing, reflection, summarising and giving of feedback are all basic coaching requirements. They are essential for building trust and rapport as most clients, even if they are the instigators of the search for coaching, will experience some ambivalence about the coaching process in the early stages. By demonstrating these aspects of a good relationship, coaches are also modelling for their client ways of becoming more professionally effective when dealing with their staff.

4

Coaching for specific business issues

Having spent the last chapter exploring what works in coaching in general, it is time to dive into some applications specific to business coaching. Rather than a detailed précis of what to do in each business situation, we have preferred to consider three broad themes: business personalities, business stages and business skills. The first refers to who we are and how we feel when in business. The second focuses on career stages and how the nature of coaching interventions varies as we move from junior, specialised positions to more experienced ones. Finally, we look at coaching as an effective way to plug gaps in the toolkit needed to succeed in business.

We adopt the same approach as previously: a description of what the issue is, of what works – illustrated by examples – and referring the reader to the extensive bibliography after the appendices.

Coaching the business personality

We do not all turn from Dr Jekyll into Mr Hyde when we walk into an office, but the work environment creates its own pressures and distortions, which means that standard life coaching approaches are unlikely to be sufficient. We start with the most common and misunderstood workplace distortion: stress.

Coaching for stress

Evidence of the damaging effects of stress has been growing for decades now. Every year the figures go up. Reports currently state that one person in five would describe themselves as very stressed at work. Sickness absence and the resultant permanent health claims are increasing. At the same time, *presenteeism* – where people feel they cannot afford to take time off work when they are suffering genuine ill health – is, according to a recent report in the *Harvard Business Review* (Hemp 2004), dwarfing direct medical costs through reduced productivity. There is therefore a direct link between stress and loss of overall good performance. A report by Sedgewick (now part of Marsh) in the 1990s described missed opportunity as one of the biggest unseen costs to business. Concomitantly, litigation has also risen, with stress cited increasingly as a cause of breakdown of health and performance. Employers have a duty of care and are expected to abide by health and safety guidelines. In the UK, employers are legally obliged to deal with stress once it has been identified; perhaps a good reason why so many British companies are terrified to even mention the S word . . . When organisations do address stress, it is often as a 'sheep dip' to teach a certain staff grade about general stress management techniques. This has a value, because we need regular reminders about the benefits of sensible exercise and diet, good behavioural practice such as planning and prioritisation and sources of relaxation. However, many executives see those as a 'nice to have' and they are rapidly neglected.

What is stress? What are its sources?

Stress is seen as a response to an excess of pressure – i.e. more than the individual can cope with. In modern business, change is one of the few constants. More and more initiatives and innovations follow at a faster pace than ever before, testing resilience to the limit.

By their very nature, senior managers are often quite driven people, insensitive to signs of wear and tear in themselves. Examples of the more benign physical symptoms which people often ignore are indigestion, headaches and sleep disturbance. They dismiss these as normal rather than the early warning signs of stress. They may have noticed their emotions are a bit more volatile, becoming short-tempered quickly or feeling despairing at times. Behaviour may have changed. They are more withdrawn than usual, avoiding social occasions or rushing faster and faster, but achieving less. Intellectually they may have noticed that their thinking is not as clear, their memories are serving them less well and that decision-making has slowed down. Frequently, however, a stressed individual may well be the last person to notice what is happening to them.

When we think of stress, we usually blame others: an excessive workload, unrealistic deadlines, responsibility without authority or lack of resources in an organisation so lean it is positively anorexic are common complaints. However, a large proportion of stress is internally generated. For example, excessive perfectionism is a common executive characteristic; this inevitably leads to a constant sense of failure or of only being as good as the last success.

The role of one-to-one coaching

One-to-one work is the only effective way to help clients interpret *signals* that can be stressful or not. As a basic example, consider noise in the middle of the night: the sound of a car at three in the morning can be seen as a stressor, unless it indicates the safe return of a teenager from a party. In this respect saying that noise is a stressor misses the point. Turning to a business example, consider the stress linked to giving an important presentation. A survey some years ago asked people to rate their fears. Speaking in public was rated higher than fear of death itself! There are many people in organisations giving presentations regularly who put themselves through the heart-racing, dry-mouthed agony of it without recognising that it could all be different. They just know that giving presentations is stressful and so avoid thinking about it until absolutely necessary. Repeat this experience often enough and you have a very stressed person. On the other hand, consider the following example.

A recent client had a high anxiety about presentations. She started agonising months ahead of presentations to the Global Board of her multinational corporation, worrying about what the effect would be if she weren't good enough. She predicted she would fail and bring her department into disrepute; other senior executives would dismiss her as incompetent and on and on. She could have done a presentation course but when we tested the evidence and asked her to present to us, she was eloquent and passionate, delivering a clear and positive message. Her own lack of confidence in her abilities was creating stress through anticipatory anxiety, preventing her from enjoying the opportunity to sound her own trumpet and receive praise for her results. Coaching therefore focused on challenging beliefs, changing behaviours and building confidence with a very minor and secondary focus on learning techniques for the final excellent presentation.

The business coach will typically use a broad array of approaches and techniques when dealing with stress. The 'draw the picture' component will focus on gathering a lot of objective data on sources of stress as well as the client's typical way of handling difficult situations. The 'achieve change' component is likely to focus on building resilience, challenging beliefs, installing new behaviours and perhaps equipping the client with a 'rescue pack' of relaxation techniques.

Stress has a very destructive impact on the individual. It also constitutes a considerable risk to the organisation if left unchecked. At best, someone senior performing under par for any length of time constitutes a serious business cost. At worst, there is a risk of errors being made, relationships deteriorating irrevocably and failure to retain very talented people. Stressed individuals should seek support through one-to-one coaching.

Coaching difficult people

Apropos specific stressors, those labelled as 'difficult people' often generate stress for themselves and others. Our definition is those persons whose style and behaviour, while allowing them to get so far in the organisation, is recognised as inappropriate and creates a virtual 'glass ceiling' to their advancement. This is particularly problematic when the difficult person is in the most senior position in their part of the organisation. There may be an absence of real feedback and no one may feel confident about being in the position to help them gain the insight that their performance, and that of the business, could be improved by coaching. In the case of the powerful owner-operator of the business, career progress is not the issue but the organisation is likely to lose its best people and simply lose business over time.

In the early days, people were often referred to coaching because of perceived difficulties or shortcomings that had not responded to more traditional training methods. Sometimes it was seen as a last ditch resort for dealing with those who might otherwise have no place in the business. An external mentor or a non-executive chairman may be able to make the recommendation but it can be a delicate business with particular implications for the initial stages of coaching.

Key elements of coaching

Even more than in most coaching the early stages of the process are critical. Difficult people often have no notion of the impact their behavioural style is having on others and thus have little recognition of their need for coaching. Others may be perfectly aware that the talents that have stood them in good stead so far in their career are no longer as productive in their new circumstances. In both groups there is, however, likely to be a defensiveness and a desire to justify the way they behave. This can make them resistant to change. For some it can be a great relief to be able to admit that they feel ill equipped for their new role and the changed demands upon them.

Analysis of the issues is likely to reveal that specific behaviours cause most irritation and resistance within the organisation. This will often be spelled out in people's 360° feedback. Clear examples are often necessary to make a convincing argument for change.

The types of issues that have occurred over the years in this category have been extremely varied: one client – managing director of an electronics manufacturer – had a tendency to take people by the throat when annoyed; another micro-managed to the utter demotivation of his direct – and very senior – reports; another had outrageously unprofessional displays of emotion in one form or another which he would attempt to correct by the equally irrational distribution of discretionary bonuses and promotions. In general many would exhibit ill-mannered behaviour as well as patronising and inappropriate treatment of others different from themselves – whether by gender, race, religion or even technical discipline.

These people probably did not wake up in the morning and plan how to be difficult that day. They are often highly focused and results-driven. It usually transpires that 'difficult' people are also highly motivated. They care passionately about outcomes but, by using approaches likely to cause others to resist them, may end up highly frustrated.

Once they have gained awareness of the impact of their specific behaviour and the likely unhelpful outcomes, coaching is likely to focus on the learning of new, more productive behaviours. The throat-crushing MD mentioned above found the proposed new communication techniques for dealing with his emotions towards a member of staff's incompetence interesting but felt where there was little time his old techniques worked most efficiently. 'It's all very well but I don't have the time for all this communication,' he said. Undaunted, the coach asked the client to role-play on video the scenario using his old aggressive style of communication and then to replay it using the new effective style. When the MD discovered that, in fact, the new version took less time, he was convinced to at least test out the effectiveness of this reformed way of behaving.

Bullies, research would tell us, do it not because they do not know any better but rather because it is fast, it is fun and it works. While most coaches might want to intervene at a deeper level – reassessing values and beliefs about people – sometimes coaching just needs to focus on helping people find equally fast and effective but less destructive ways of behaving.

Coaching stars

At the opposite end of the human spectrum, some clients are genuine stars. Although coaching usually purports to be about developing rather than problem-solving, it can be daunting to coach those who seem to be really very good already. There can be a risk of trying too hard to ensure they are getting their money's worth! A client of ours is a walking embodiment of good leadership. He is confident, personable. He knows all his directors, their families and children. He has a great home life and supportive family. Although he works hard, he rarely misses sailing opportunities at the weekend with friends and his grown-up sons. Several times a week he will just down tools and head for the gym for an hour knowing that his mind will be clearer for problem-solving on his return. If he considers someone does not fit with the culture he is building or does not share his ethics, he will deal with it at once, removing the person if necessary. He is decisive and doesn't worry unduly about making mistakes. 'What's the worst they could do?' he asks. 'Fire me? More time for sailing!' So why is he regularly devoting some of his precious time to coaching? He describes it as his sanity check, time out where he can consider and be challenged by someone with impartiality. Coaching provides an opportunity to keep checking that he is looking to the big picture and not being sucked under by constant daily demands. It also means that he does not get a chance to rest on his laurels and coast. If he is not enjoying his role he expects to be challenged about where the next step in life may take him.

It is very easy for the good performer to be left well alone in an almost superstitious fear of jinxing how well they are doing. Yet we know that constant development and realignment are an important part of high performance. More companies are becoming aware of this and as a result are attempting to identify and access potential high performers and provide them with coaching throughout each stage of their career.

Coaching men

With 70 per cent of senior executives being men, it may seem odd to look at them as a separate group needing specific interventions. Perhaps a better description would be: 'successful men who have a traditional career progression'. They tend to be highly intelligent, independent, driven and outwardly extremely confident. Others think of them as 'natural leaders' who operate to a high level of performance, achieve success through action-oriented determination and have a highly developed sense of responsibility. They have often achieved greater wealth at a younger age than their fathers, or other family members, ever did. This can be significant. They will have driven themselves to this point but may encounter a *crisis of meaning* once they have reached the top (*coaching for meaning* is covered later in this chapter).

Why would such a group embark on coaching? With a blend of attributes which almost guarantees them personal success comes a range of characteristics which may in turn limit their full potential. For instance, they automatically expect the same drive from everyone around them, taking extreme commitment and levels of performance for granted. Seriously data-driven, they may have shown little curiosity on their way up about the human side of things and as a result miss seeing the whole picture. They may also blindly underestimate how important their every word and action is to those around them. Consequently, they miss opportunities to motivate and they may fail to inspire people to follow in their footsteps. Others may see their sacrifice as too great or their standards as too unachievable to emulate. They are unlikely to admit to problems and traditionally do not ask for help.

Without being consciously aware of it, many of their values come from much earlier times. Someone successful today probably shares many values with his Victorian grandfather. These values are useful in driving the work ethic but may, if unrecognised, lead to other problems later. The fact that those coming up through the organisation behind them have absorbed the beliefs of a post-war or even 1960s set of ancestors means that values are not automatically shared. They may have come from a background where men did the work or had the professions and spent their lives, man and boy, providing for families till their retirement at 65. In contrast, their own lives are likely to be quite different. While their predecessors may have earned respect in their roles, especially where hard labour and sacrifice are concerned, current successful men live in different circumstances. They may be part of a dual career household where respect will not be automatically given for having a career, or they may have struck a bargain with a partner that has allowed them to focus single-mindedly on their career while she has dealt, often alone, with all the other aspects of their existence. This can have a marginalising effect on men in the home.

Key elements of coaching

In order for such a person to engage in coaching, self-awareness is a prerequisite. This man will not want to sit around contemplating himself for long, so quantifiable data from 360° feedback from those in the organisation is vital. Clear evidence of the impact of his actions needs to be presented in the form of hard and irrefutable data in order to make an impression.

Coaches themselves have to be particularly skilled and adaptive when dealing with such a client. Experience of working at this level, a capacity to speak the client's language and an ability to be analytical are all important assets. It is also essential not to be overwhelmed by the client's status.

Coaches should employ direct and often challenging confrontation with reality.

Data presented in the form of a well thought out business case is likely to be the most effective. In order to engage the client, the coach should not hesitate to replay his traditional values – e.g. courage, sacrifice and striving for results – in order to ensure that he gets a sense of duty in seeing the process through to tangible results.

Coaching women

While stereotypes can be invidious and often wrong, there is still a case for reviewing women separately. We will not repeat here discussions on glass ceilings and walls or the concept of 'pink collar jobs': those roles almost designated exclusively for women either because the culture appeals more to them or because they have been deemed a more appropriate choice.

While the change for men has been largely one of values and careers compared to the previous generation, as seen above, women's careers have been transformed in absolutely all areas. Although many women have always worked and been required to do so to raise their families over the centuries, the possibility of entering professions and rising through business organisations is startlingly recent. Confident teenage schoolgirls today express little doubt about their ability to hold their own and succeed in areas that not so long ago were considered 'a man's world'. Hard-fought battles through the 1960s and 1970s ensured a woman's right to choose a profession but the journey to equality has had its very rough patches and it is questionable whether women have arrived yet.

More interestingly, it would appear that many women who embarked on the corporate journey have decided that they wanted to go somewhere else. This is not because the terrain was too difficult for them, but that their values and priorities lay elsewhere. This is more than anecdotal: women, for example, constitute 62 per cent of law graduates in the UK, but only 23 per cent of partners and 10 per cent of partners in big city firms.

While pioneering women in the past had very few role models to inspire them, men had many, but all from very similar moulds. Women now have far greater choice than they ever had. This can give them flexibility and choice in planning more adaptive careers. While 'house husbands' now exist in greater numbers than before, there is a greater likelihood that a woman will either be single, with or without dependants, or in a relationship with another breadwinner. Consequently they may have greater choice and freedom and therefore less deep-down belief in the institution they inhabit as the only true source of their success.

Women, given the opportunity to enter coaching, may be more likely to do so for several reasons. Although they often have better social networks and may be more used to discussing issues at a personal level, women have often had far less access to business mentors than men. They are also less likely to perceive the process of receiving help as a weakness.

Key elements of coaching

One dilemma for many women is whether, upon entering a male-dominated organisation, to adopt the accepted styles and standards of behaviour even if they do not feel appropriate or even professional. It was once considered essential to 'outman the men' in behaviour, style and in disregard for any concept of work-life balance. In some instances this possibly led to women making the choice either not to marry or not to have children. Otherwise there can often be an unspoken question about their real commitment, despite the fact that men change jobs more frequently than women. Coaching can help a woman examine what impact she wants to have on an organisation, how she needs to be perceived and how she may need to modify her behaviour.

Developing an appropriate professional style depends on initial self-awareness, accurate understanding of strengths and weaknesses and how they are presently perceived by others. The sexes are often judged differently on a number of issues so it is important for a woman to take stock of what messages she is giving and how she wants to modify them in a corporate setting. A coach can also help her explore the unwritten rules and games that are played within the organisation, so that she can determine how best to deal with these. Letitia, in Chapter 6, sought out coaching because she realised that she was not competent at playing an essentially political game which would be vital to her career advancement.

Women often expect to be recognised and rewarded for doing a good job and overlook the need to showcase themselves. In fact they can be disparaging about those who 'blow their own trumpet'. (Whose would you blow?) Coaching addresses their visibility in the business by examining and changing how they create their own image, speak up in more daunting situations and take credit when they have done good work.

Much of the specific coaching focus should therefore be on communication and presence. For example, women smile much more than men, sometimes in an inappropriately conciliatory fashion. This can detract from the power of the message they are imparting. Physically smaller in many instances, they can take up less room than their male counterparts and often have to work to build presence and gravitas. When tense, their voices tend to become higher and they run the risk of being labelled shrill. Although the woman herself may be boundlessly confident, coaching may have to focus on ensuring that that message gets across. This has to be achieved while remaining true to herself and her style, not distorted or over 'elocutionised' like some past politicians.

However, many women are not as confident as their performance should imply. With a certain diffidence, they have failed to 'accumulate value' as they have progressed. The outward trappings and display of success are often of less interest, causing their male counterparts to misjudge their achievements.

One of our clients, head of global HR in the entertainment industry, found herself feeling increasingly minimised at board meetings and began to doubt her contribution and ability. By studying how her male colleagues gained the attention of the room, she gradually saw the need to alter her consultative and conciliatory style to communicate the force of her arguments more strongly. For many women this is a delicate procedure as women's behaviours are judged differently from men's. A businesswoman making a tough decision is still seen as going against her sex, while a comparable man will be applauded for taking a difficult decision.

Coaching at different career stages

One-to-one work is useful at every stage of a business career, but we have found through experience that specific interventions should be designed for key career stages. Here we focus on the main events in a businessperson's life: the big promotion, coaching for leadership and coaching for meaning.

The big promotion

Many of our clients experience coaching for the first time when getting ready for a major promotion: this can be before making it to partner in a law or accounting firm; switching from a specialised function such as finance or engineering to a general management role; or simply moving from a business delivery to a business management role. They may ask for coaching to support their fast career development, or they may be missing one of the key characteristics of the new job. They may be difficult people (see above), may have a gap in their skills (see below) or may miss the elusive quality of 'gravitas' required by senior people. In many cases, they will be terrified of leaving the familiarity of being on top of their game in their old role, to become 'one of them'. This is particularly true in professional services firms, where there is often a marked difference of status and treatment between partners and non-partners.

This is one of the areas where one-to-one coaching can make a huge and rapid difference. In most professions – and we shall use this as a metaphor for all industries – gravitas had to be acquired over years, rubbing shoulders with partners, observing them in action with clients and generally picking up tips through informal mentoring. With the end of apprenticeship as described in Chapter 1, new partners are expected to acquire these skills overnight, without any formal preparation. Most newly-promoted partners we know spend a very uncomfortable two years and can be seriously dysfunctional.

Key elements of coaching

Coaching for this group should be focused on accelerating development and generally covers the following areas:

- Confidence
- Personal impact
- Managing emotions
- Communications
- Coaching others
- Thinking style
- Planning work
- Ongoing development

In other words, newly-promoted executives need a mix of our ITEA model shown in Chapter 2 with a good dose of business contextualisation. This can produce stunning results. One recent example was that of a newly-promoted partner who was floundering commercially, simply because she did not have the confidence to 'let go' of her former role as an excellent technical project manager. Working on her confidence, the impact she made on fellow partners and in designing a precise business plan that included many confidence-boosting early wins was sufficient to make her perform beyond the partner median within 12 months.

Coaching for leadership

Coaching can be a very useful approach to unlock leadership potential as is now used in high-flying leadership executive development courses in leading business schools.

The ingredients are similar to those in other forms of coaching: self-awareness, understanding what motivates (senior) people, thinking styles (using cognitive-behavioural approaches) and creating delivery roadmaps. The difference is in the extreme flexibility needed by the coach to jump from highly personal agendas to technical boardroom issues. Two recent examples illustrate this: one client was leading the scientific team of a global consumer goods company. She was successful but constantly doubting her ability to lead her group. It all came down to exploring beliefs between success and having a happy family. Obviously the techniques used to reframe her beliefs in this case were not different from what an experienced life coach would use. In another case, a client was seen by fellow board members as unsophisticated and doubted his ability to interface with the City in a credible manner. We designed and implemented with him a multiple approach of personal development (including impact on colleagues), presentation coaching, complex project management and objective-setting over six months. This 'high octane' approach produced rapid results and he is now running most of the US businesses, dealing with American stock analysts in the process – perhaps the most visible testimony of his achievements.

So is coaching for leadership simply a more complex version of regular business coaching? We think that there are some significant differences, illustrated by the paradoxes of the leader's role.

Paradox 1: the wrong skill set

The skills required to get to the top are often 180° opposed to those required to be a successful leader. Reliable delivery, attention to detail and teamwork all become less important once in a position of visible leadership. They are replaced by vision, communication and motivation, for example. Although this is an imperfect list (there are many more models of leadership than the visionary or charismatic leader), it illustrates how uncomfortable the new position can be. Obviously, coaching can be of great help in objectively assessing which new skills are required and ensuring that development takes place at the right pace.

Paradox 2: omnipotent expertise

Put simply, everybody expects you to have all the answers all the time, both inside and outside the company. Many new leaders are not prepared for the sudden increase in pressure, especially if they originate from a specialist area. Again, coaching can help, be it for handling stress, priorities, building the right team or communicating with all stakeholders.

Paradox 3: it is truly lonely at the top

But this is not a quiet form of loneliness: the new leader is constantly immersed in conversations with people who all have an agenda. The coach's primary role is that of a neutral sounding board. The key skill in this context is to know when to share one's own business experience and when to act as a simple mirror to the client. The coach should be very clear in the signposting of interventions: the worst that can happen is for a coach to replay his own business life through helping a new leader!

Coaching for meaning

Coaching has a huge impact when people reach the stage of questioning the purpose and value of what they are doing and contemplating later stages of their careers. Senior executives have usually worked with focus and determination to achieve success in business. They spent the first part of their lives training for success and the next stage working hard to achieve it. For many, the time then comes when they wonder, 'Is this it?' Somehow the satisfaction they had expected is less rich than they had hoped for and does not have the power to motivate them for the next stage of their lives. In a sense, they are bored, but they often also begin to question whether they still value what they are doing. One client actually said – and this was not bragging – 'I just don't need the next half-million pound bonus; it doesn't do it for me any more.' Sometimes it is clear that by climbing steadily up the corporate ladder, they have narrowed their options and interests and perhaps lost the opportunity to use some of their key strengths.

This is also often true for the successful entrepreneur who, having conceived the business idea and having pursued the dream relentlessly, is now in charge of an established and successful business with no apparent exit route. Strongly identified with the business it may seem impossible to move on.

For others sometimes there is a nagging, 'but I always wanted to be a . . . doctor, teacher, dancer, whatever' and a sense of lack of fulfilment. When we talked to a number of human resources professionals, they all recognised this condition. In fact quite a few were experiencing it themselves at the time!

There is a high risk that people will embark on random changes in their lives – taking an unpredictable horizontal move, giving up their job and moving to the country or embarking on an affair. It is at this stage that people will often say something like, 'I think I'll teach.' The notion is of doing good, doing something meaningful even if it turns out that they are deeply unsuited to it. The risk to business is the unplanned, unexpected loss of the best people when they are at their most valuable. The risk to the individual is that of making bad, ill-considered choices or staying in a job which no longer excites, becoming increasingly disaffected as a result. In the past this stage was often referred to as a mid-life crisis. The crises are now happening younger and younger while people are staying fitter longer and becoming wealthier earlier. The puzzle is how to use this opportunity not available to many in previous generations.

Key elements of coaching

There can be a tendency to equate mid-life interrogation with the need for a long holiday or psychotherapy. Our approach is simpler, more direct and genuinely linked to the success of both the individual and the business.

- *Reviewing the past*

   Coaching gives the opportunity to take stock of the big picture. For years the focus will have been within the business context. A total life and career review with particular emphasis on what made the good times so good will identify the essential components of the next stage.

Research from the field of positive psychology has established that for true happiness, people need to live meaningful lives. Wealth and material possessions alone do not contribute significantly to happiness and well-being. Using key strengths and being connected to something larger than yourself are vital components of the pursuit of life satisfaction. At this stage, clients often recognise that they no longer use the skills they have enjoyed using most and can begin to determine what they feel is an essential requirement for the future.

- *Testing realities*

  People can be unrealistic about either the difficulties or the ease with which they might either change direction or find challenge again in their current role. This stage focuses on beliefs which might prevent them from making a success of the next stage of their lives. Testing the evidence for the beliefs gives the opportunity to assess how achievable their goals are. Careful consideration must be given to all the factors, from financial implications to family attitudes, which must be addressed in order to make the transition. At this stage consultation with other relevant advisers such as accountants or lawyers will contribute to the efficacy of the process.

- *Planning for action*

  In the past, clients will no doubt have been involved in careful business planning. They deserve just the same professionalism in planning their career. At this stage they can carefully assess the robustness of their plan while supported by their coach.

Coaching for business skills

Some specific business coaching applications relate to acquiring the specific skills needed to perform well in a business environment. The most common are:

- Selling
- Presenting

- Managing multiple projects
- Motivating others

The most obvious question is: why should a coaching approach be required in areas where literally thousands of courses exist? In coaching fashion, we would reply to the reader with another question: what proportion of the training you ever took resulted in durable behavioural change?

We know from experience that most people who don't sell much actually have issues with the idea of selling, not with selling techniques. Similarly those who think they present poorly may have a fairly low level of confidence, a 'don't brag' upbringing or think that ideas expressed on paper should speak for themselves. In other words, we believe that most training courses fail because they act mainly at the conscious cognitive level but fail to take into account our motivation, our beliefs and generally the lack of connection between knowing something and actually acting on it.

There are many approaches to working both at the conscious and unconscious levels with clients, from various schools of therapy (say, psychodynamics or Gestalt) to hypnotic communications or a whole host of techniques concerning values and beliefs derived from neuro-linguistic programming. We think that there are three keys to success in coaching for business skills: content, awareness and flexibility.

Content

There is plenty of good available content in all specialised skills areas and the business coach will need to master the main ones, preferably by being formally qualified. It is important that the coach should be aware of what is used in the corporate world. In sales for instance, most large British organisations have used or at least heard about 'SPIN selling'.

The coach needs to be ready to offer plain 'vanilla' training, either one-to-one or to a group if that is what the client wants. In many cases though, the standard training approaches have already been tried but have failed to produce results, which leads us to our next point.

Awareness and flexibility

Clients usually have a good awareness of the limited usefulness of standard training and will also have beliefs generally concerning being good or bad at a certain skills area. A skilled coach will use this opportunity to reframe and generally shake the beliefs of the client in a supportive and constructive way. Many highly 'logical' clients may have difficulty with beliefs held at the 'less-than-conscious' level however, and the first stage of discovery for such clients should be the inescapable conclusion that 'there is something else': after all, if a skill could simply be learned at the conscious level, then these intelligent and driven individuals would have done it a long time ago. The coach's role is also obviously to introduce the notion that they have a choice about becoming excellent in any skills area.

The next challenge in coaching for skills is to find a type and style of intervention that is appropriate for the client: a business coach can lose all credibility if they launch into techniques which come across as too 'exotic'. In our experience, there is no way to test the receptiveness of a client to such techniques based on background or even work area: for instance, a client who responded extremely well to regression and Gestalt is a very formal and detailed 'back office/settlement' specialist whose work life is governed by facts, not emotions. Our recommendation is therefore to tread carefully before trying something new. Most clients are highly curious and hate being manipulated. They therefore respond very well when presented with a theoretical introduction to a new approach: after all, we are the experts and they generally listen to us the same way they would listen to a trusted colleague from another functional area.

One-to-one or groups?

To be blunt, there is a scale difference between signing up someone on a course and contracting for a coaching programme. The economics change significantly however when a group of executives is coached in a certain skill and when a mixed approach of group and one-to-one work is chosen.

Group work is not only about reducing cost; it is also about utilising group learning and group dynamics. It is particularly enlightening for example for a group of individuals to discover that they all have a similar 'weakness' or doubt in a given technical area. It creates the right set-up for creative problem-solving. Groups generally represent a safe environment provided that confidentiality is managed carefully.

We recommend mixing one-to-one and group work to facilitate long-term learning. Data from one-to-one sessions can be sanitised and shared at the next group sessions for example. At the same time individuals' beliefs and priorities can be incorporated into personal action plans that will maximise the chances of successful behaviour installation.

In conclusion

We have detailed what we see as the specific applications of business coaching: business personalities, business stages and business skills. Any new client will straddle several of those. They will test the business coach in terms of breadth, depth and flexibility. No client should expect an individual coach to be able to deliver such a broad agenda.

The consequence is that business coaches should have a clear awareness of their comfort zone and ally themselves with other experts to cover the whole gamut of business interventions. If coaches need to pool their skills, what is the best format to do so: loose alliances or employment in large firms? To find out, we asked large companies how and why they purchased coaching, and this is developed in the next chapter.

Conversations with sponsors

We cannot constantly ask our clients to get objective feedback and not heed our own advice. The value of coaching is ultimately decided by those who receive it and who fund it. Best practice is what works for the client, not necessarily the most elegant psychological construct. So we went out and asked clients what they thought. This chapter focuses on corporate sponsors: collectively they have gone through at least two, sometimes three cycles of buying and evaluating coaching. What have they found out? How will they purchase and evaluate business coaching in the future?

This chapter will be highly relevant to HR professionals who want to compare notes, to coaches who want to offer more relevant services, and to would-be coaches who can hone-in their preparation. The next chapter drills down into the individual coaching experience.

We had detailed conversations with five multinationals during the second half of 2004: BT (telecoms), Group 4 Securicor (security), PricewaterhouseCoopers (audit), Scottish Power (utility) and a major European bank. Some are our clients; all have more than one supplier of coaching services. The conversations were candid and are reported with as little editing as possible so that readers pick up the implicit messages. In each case we have asked the interviewees to supply words of wisdom based on their experience: first what they would advise other companies to do when selecting suppliers and ensuring that their clients get the best possible results; then we asked them for advice for coaches themselves. We draw conclusions at the end of the chapter.

BT – 'the end of the beginning'

The company

BT Group plc is the result of one of the major privatisations of the 1980s. Its principal activities include telephony, data services, consulting, and IT operations. It is a large (£19 billion), mainly British, company; and each of its five divisions would be a large business in its own right. Although each division has its own dedicated HR services, there is also a group HR function which takes the lead on group-wide HR strategy and programmes.

Coaching at BT

Between five and seven years ago, executive coaching was largely seen as a remedial process for senior people in the organisation, aimed at overcoming serious problems that had not proved possible to 'fix' by any other means. There was probably something wrong with you if you had a coach.

About five years ago, Liz Wallace, talent director, began to see a shift in the market. Having a coach became more of a fashion statement. Suddenly, through word of mouth, as people began to talk about how good an experience it could be, coaching took off. It spread like a virus, without being a planned addition to development portfolios. Budgets were with the line so coaching was both self-motivated and self-purchased. As a decentralised organisation BT did not actively control either quantity or quality. There was no way of tracking what might appear under the guise of consultancy, coaching or training and development. Nor did Liz have any particular will to control it at that stage. Putting control in too early was, she thought, likely to be a potentially limiting mistake.

By 2003 coaching was being used extensively among the top 250 people – the top couple of layers of the executive. More and more coaching companies were pitching to BT but little was known about what was being commissioned. Two concerns emerged – quality and good commercialism. The quality of the coaching became a cause for some anxiety. Media coverage about the dangers of poor coaching and an increase in individuals having negative experiences necessitated better understanding and control. Commercial issues centred on the fact that there was no account of how large sums of money were being spent. It was felt essential to get a grip and find ways of maximising value.

An extensive study was undertaken through the HR community to flush out and map the use of coaching. A working group of ten was set up across the organisation, including HR and line. The team operated across functions and businesses. Using the International Coach Federation (ICF) criteria the team defined what they were looking for from coaching. Coaches did not have to be ICF qualified nor was the ICF considered better than other organisations. It was just a place to start the process. Using competencies as a base, they first asked coaches to talk about their own skills and competencies using ICF as a term of reference. They reviewed the coach's track record. Did they have experience with a wide range of blue-chip companies or just this one? How committed were they to continual professional development? They asked about professional qualifications but were not dogmatic about the requirements. The range was wide from psychologists to neuro-linguistic programming practitioners. This process provided sufficient data for an initial paper sift. As a result, 30 organisations were invited to present to the team bringing no more than three people to the presentation. BT buys coaches not organisations so there was no specific advantage in being part of a large company. Only coaches who actually presented would be considered, which levelled the playing field for people from a range of companies. The setting was formal and some coaches did not present well. In a semi-formal setting, a few coaches also committed the cardinal sin of trying to coach rather than pitch. A portfolio of 40 individual coaches from around 25 organisations was selected.

A launch was held for the coaches. Talent leaders and business partners who would be in a position to make recommendations were also invited, giving them the opportunity to meet the coaches face to face. Many coaches also appreciated the opportunity to meet other coaches as they often work alone. The top 250 people in the company were sent information about the coaches and a website was set up to advertise the service and the suppliers. A database of the coaches was established. It contains brief résumés, price bands and category or specialty of their coaching. BT is now confident about the quality of the coaching provided but the project team will conduct six-monthly reviews to establish whether the quantity is sufficient. Coaching now has to go through procurement to be allocated a code. This ensures that people are unable to use non-preferred suppliers and also enables the company to track the spend.

Anarchy has gradually been brought under control but is unlikely to be totally controlled in such a large organisation. The main aims now are to assess whether someone needs a coach, to help them find the right one and to give them the tools to make sure they get the best out of the experience. Coaches are provided with a set of guidelines and there are feedback forms for both coach and their client.

A three-sided relationship is recommended to include the coach, their client and the sponsor who could be either their line manager or the budget holder. Objectives are set, with the sponsoring manager's involvement, to be achieved within a six-month time scale. Coaching is reviewed on the basis of these objectives, which form part of the contract with the organisation. Coaches are expected to manage confidentiality but to feed back appropriately within the review and the agreed objectives.

The aim is to treat people like adults with a sense of maturity and responsibility. At the same time BT wish to be very responsive to any whiff of things not going right and to quickly take action to rectify as necessary. At the six-monthly reviews with the coach, there is an update on BT strategy which is likely to impact on clients. Coaches are expected to feed back emerging themes and to give an insight into any trends they see developing.

Liz describes the point they have now reached, in Winston Churchill's famous words of 1942, as 'the end of the beginning'. Coaching may now have reached a plateau and be about to hit a second wave. After early adopters, coaching is now becoming mainstream at BT and cascading down through the organisation.

Words of wisdom

With all that insight, here are Liz's tips for businesses introducing coaching and for would be business coaches.

For businesses:

1 Involve both HR and line people who are ultimate customers of coaching in the process of picking coaches. Not only will you get valuable insight into the range of requirements in your organisation but you will also ensure buy-in into the final list of coaches you choose.
2 Be clear about the criteria you are going to adopt to evaluate coaches. There is no right answer so pick the criteria that work best for your business and stick to them.
3 Take time to meet as many coaches as needed so as to fulfil your criteria before making your final decision – there is no substitute for meeting a coach face to face.

And for coaches:

1 Qualifications are critical as they are often the baseline for evaluation. That said, it is more your commitment to continual professional development than particular qualifications that matters.
2 Pitching to an organisation may not come naturally to you as it is a very different interaction than coaching. If you are uncomfortable about it, get some help from a fellow coach and practise!
3 Build a strong portfolio of client testimonials and if possible get at least a couple to agree to speak to prospective customers for you. Personal recommendation is a powerful tool and may help differentiate you.

Group 4 Securicor – 'information rich and integrated'

The company

Group 4 Securicor is the result of the July 2004 merger that amalgamated three major security brands: Group 4, Wackenhut and Securicor. The company focuses on three major businesses: manned security (e.g. premises, airports, transporting prisoners), security systems (monitoring) and cash services (fund transport). In addition to traditional services, the company has also invested in a number of related businesses, from security at sporting events to outsourcing prison management, or to running ATM networks on behalf of banks. Group 4 Securicor is present in over 100 countries (⅔ of the business is in Europe) and turns over about £4 billion.

This interview took place at the time of the merger and focuses mainly on the Securicor business.

Coaching at Group 4 Securicor

It really all began in the summer of 1998. The chief executive had been approached by some of the well-known coaching houses looking for business. He spoke to the group HR director about whether they should be commissioning coaching for senior executives. At much the same time Mike Alsop, having completed his masters in management development, was involved in 'development needs identification'. In effect this was coaching – entailing a great deal of careful questioning, listening and understanding of individual requirements. Mike describes himself at this point as novice, working a little outside of the fold.

Development at Securicor prior to this point had involved partnerships with organisations such as The Institute of Directors and a provision of group programmes. Although these had value, at the time a 'one size fits all' approach felt like a waste. An individualistic, tailored approach was envisaged. So Mike was asked by the three divisional HR directors to send a number of coaching organisations an invitation to tender as there were three individuals in the organisation to be coached at that point. As this process seemed a little extreme and overly formal, they were just asked to come and talk. The beauty parade process began. However, nothing further happened then for a number of reasons: coaching looked very expensive; there seemed to be no way to measure the process; and confidentiality looked like an issue. A great deal of thought then went into the process until it evolved to its current state.

Developing their people is seen as a big part of most senior line executives' responsibility. The process commences with a lengthy annual review of each of the direct reports. Mike as head of executive development will meet with the senior executive often for as much as three days to review all available data. This will include all psychometric measures, ability test scores, annual career and review documents, Securicor-specific 360° feedback, including as a prerequisite detailed self-report and any other available data. Each individual reviewed may have been assessed on a different range of measures but the discussions are based on the company competency model to ensure consistency throughout. The performance management documentation for the last year will be studied to assess whether the agreed targets were achieved. 'Grandparents' views' – impressions from the chief executive or similar – will be sought.

This generates a considerable volume of both quantitative and qualitative data, not necessarily like-for-like between all individuals being reviewed but a very rich source of information and impression. There is a sophisticated and intense use of all aspects of measurement, including intuitive reactions which Mike is at pains to point out could not be further from 'fluffy thinking' but in fact involves checking the heart, head and gut feelings concerning the individual.

A mind map is then generated as a means of capturing all the data on each individual in one place and as a catalytic starter for the next phase of dialogue with the boss about his direct reports. Once the conversation starts, then themes emerge clearly. The process is highly pragmatic, defining needs along the lines of:

- What this person could do more of
- What they should do less of
- What they should do differently

Interestingly, this entire process is conducted using a coaching approach. Mike uses strong listening and questioning skills but also relies on observational techniques to pick up on underlying concerns or doubts that the senior executive may not be consciously addressing. Once both parties are happy at having mined the information from the data and evolved the final plan, proposals are made for how the development issues may be addressed. A personal development report is compiled using a standard template, which encapsulates the development need, the proposal and the time frame for achievement. Links are made to the related competency in the company's framework.

It is only at this stage, once a considerable time investment has been made, that the individual is involved in the process. The development areas are always put in the context of 'broadening your repertoire' as by definition these are people who are already performing well within the company. A three-way discussion takes place for around 60–90 minutes. The process, the findings and the suggested development plan are all reviewed. A range of choices is always given for the development – which may often suggest coaching as just one of a range of interventions. These 'trialogues' are very healthy and open, allowing for challenge where the findings may prove inaccurate or inadequate. They also put the responsibility firmly with the individual for making the changes happen. The process is annualised but within that time different review periods may be established for each person depending on their development needs. At this stage it is not seen as important to be overly rigorous but three- and six-monthly reviews of coaching would be likely. People are expected to feed back to their bosses anyway about their development experiences.

As a result of this very rigorous, time-consuming and quite onerous front end, Securicor believes there is a very high likelihood of successful outcomes. The chief executive has been quoted as saying, 'You instinctively know when you are doing the right thing.' The core process has been developed to create space for people to develop in quite different ways. The managing directors find the process interesting and enjoyable. However, it has become increasingly onerous for one person in the role of head of executive development to facilitate intensively and fairly across the organisation.

With regard to the selection of possible coaches, rather than there being a closed preferred supplier list and specific criteria, there is an ongoing interest in meeting people and compiling a repository of information and opinion about the quality of coaches available. Prior to the coach meeting the client, they will meet with Mike to discuss terms, costs and feedback arrangements. Once satisfactory agreement has been reached, they will be introduced to the sponsor. If the sponsor approves, they then meet the client. From one to three coaches may be introduced and the client will choose who to commit to. The coach is required to gain some form of 360° awareness by setting up meetings with a range of colleagues to collect information and feedback about their client. This ensures commitment from all to enable the individual to achieve their targets through effective coaching. The coaching process is very open. It is not just openly known that people have coaches from the chief executive down, it is even trumpeted.

There is no formal evaluation of coaching other than consistent reviews during and at the end of the coaching. Coaching can vary from intensive 'retreat' type residential coaching through to the more usual monthly sessions. Sessions may be an hour, a half day or a day as appropriate. It is considered preferable for coaching to take place off site. There is a general expectation that people will share any development experience such as external programmes, certainly with their managers and perhaps also with colleagues. This can apply to coaching as well. On occasions people may be working with two coaches – one fundamental and the other for very specific performance aspects such as media presentation.

Where Securicor has learned from its mistakes is the area of standardising the selection and allocation process. People are discouraged from entering into individual agreements that have not been subjected to the rigorous assessment process described. This reduces the likelihood of ineffectual or misplaced coaching taking place. As a company they prefer not to enter into percentage of salary deals, expecting an equivalent standard whatever the level of client being coached.

The future for Group 4 Securicor is seen as one of mergers, acquisitions and growth. Coaching is seen as continuing to be an important element especially as it is by now extremely well understood. There is now a national and organisational comfort with coaching. The next challenge will be applying the established process outside of the UK with limited global application. A main issue will be whether to subcontract – for instance in the Far East and Asia. Another will be how to tackle widely diverse cultural issues. There is also an ongoing desire to understand the scope and efficacy of coaching. A major focus will be on how to reproduce and ensure the quality of the intensive assessment process which currently resides in the one person – Mike Alsop.

There is no set template for coaches employed by Group 4 Securicor. As a result they use a wide range of approaches. One vital requirement is that they are able to describe or demonstrate a logical process underlying their practice. The company will be looking for demonstrable and appropriate values. They would also expect the coach to have an understanding of what motivates and drives their own and others' behaviour. Coaches should be intellectually and emotionally capable of dealing with both high complexity and ambiguity. There are rarely right answers. Coaches, like the people they are coaching, need to be looking for opportunities for change rather than responding. Regulation of coaches by an independent body is seen as useful as it would raise the bar, excluding the less able or professional at the first hurdle.

Words of wisdom

With all that insight, here are Mike's tips for businesses introducing coaching and for would be business coaches.

For businesses:

1 Always make time to meet and talk with potential new coaches. There are huge numbers of people in the coaching market, all with differing approaches and techniques; it's unlikely that the first ones you meet will be absolutely 'right' for you, and it pays to have a large pool to select from.
2 Always ensure that the line manager of the person being coached is completely clear about why the coaching arrangement is being set up and how it is going to add value/improve performance.
3 Always find out how the coach goes about developing their own performance, and how they are 'supervised'.

And for coaches:

1 Be honest about what you can do and what you can't do.
2 Be clear and uncomplicated when talking to line managers about your approach and the techniques that you use.

3 Don't go quiet on the customer; keep on communicating with the company, and don't wait to be asked for an update.

PricewaterhouseCoopers – 'internal centre of excellence'

The company

PricewaterhouseCoopers (PwC) is the world's largest accounting firm. In the UK, it audits 42 of the FTSE 100 companies and also provides tax and advisory services. The UK firm (PwC LLP) belongs to 800 partners and employs about 13,000 staff. Culturally PwC has a deep understanding of professional staff development needs and coaching has been a long-standing feature on both sides of the Atlantic. This conversation focuses on practices at the UK firm.

Coaching at PwC

Dee Cullen, who heads up executive coaching at PwC LLP described the development of coaching within PwC. As she came originally from Coopers & Lybrand (C&L) this history of coaching really starts with the merger of Price Waterhouse (PW) and C&L in the late 1990s. C&L had used coaching mainly as a remedial tool. Its focus was on promotion panels or the achievement of specific goals. It had not yet been fully embraced as a positive option within a range of development options. There were two cultures with two development philosophies, out of which a new identity was crafted. New competency frameworks were developed. New ways of promoting people within the merged organisation stimulated an appetite for coaching.

A strong organisational development team assumed responsibility for coaching. Demand grew and an in-house coaching practice was developed more formally. They started by putting together their own code of practice. Then they offered coaching as a more visible service, printing their own brochure and developing an evaluation system. It was important that as an internal supplier their offering would stand up to scrutiny as being as professional as an external supplier's would be. An evaluation project was conducted to retrospectively review coaching as used in PW and C&L. This gleaned a great deal of positive feedback, validating an internal service and giving credibility to the coaching process. It also provided a baseline against which future coaching could be assessed.

There has been growth in coaching since then. Word got around. Coaching individuals became a positive choice from a range of options and processes for development. There is more of an educated buying mentality now as both professional buyers and clients in the firm are more informed and discerning as to what will add value.

A network of coaches was established. The PwC Organisation Effectiveness and Development team (OED) drew on British Association for Counselling and Psychotherapy (BACP) and British Psychological Society (BPS) guidelines for ethics and standards for supervision. Various models were tested and a variety of approaches were encouraged.

The OED coach team has always used an external coach to handle supervision. By using different models there is ongoing learning and development for coaches who wish to enrich their practice. A richness of approach and a diversity of techniques are encouraged when coaches meet to share their philosophy and practice. All are expected to operate to a high ethical standard.

The PwC Coaching Centre of Excellence (CCE), under the auspices of OED, has been established to operate like a consultancy from which internal teams buy in services. They do not have to use the internal services to provide coaching but are advised to use the CCE as a sounding board when commissioning external providers. Guidelines are provided describing the services offered, their credentials, how to access the service, how it operates and who is part of the coaching team. This balances the essential element of choice for the purchaser with the need to ensure high professional standards of provision.

The CCE provides briefing notes for the client and coach – clarifying the nature of coaching, the skills used, how the process works in the business – with a flow diagram charting the process from recognition of a need to resolution and conclusion of coaching. The CCE provides a clear and detailed code of ethics and practice for coaching within PwC. This covers ethical and political questions such as:

- Ethical: am I competent to coach this individual on this subject? Shall I refer on?
- Political: who is the client? What organisational issues are implicit in this issue and should I communicate them? What are the boundaries of confidentiality?

Operational guidelines are given for limits of work, boundaries, confidentiality, accountability, evaluation and quality control. All coaches are required to receive supervision for the type of coaching work they do and their particular needs as follows:

- One hour of supervision per minimum five hours and maximum ten hours of client work.
- Both internal supervision by experienced coaches and independent supervision by qualified external supervisors.

Record keeping is required in the form of:

- Numbers of partners and staff coached
- Line of service
- Grade
- Type of issue

Additional guidance material is provided in the form of an outline of the likely content of the first meeting, making referrals and a selection of sample forms. These include data collection, record of coaching sessions, review of progress, preparing for supervision and client questionnaire.

Coaching is usually initiated once a development issue has been identified. There could be a number of reasons for this: feedback from an appraisal or performance review, someone is earmarked as having potential as a result of 360° feedback, feedback from clients, a crossroad has been identified as a result of a training programme or as the next identified phase of development. Discussions will follow to encourage the individual to take responsibility for their own development. A mentor might be involved prior to contact with the CCE to establish whether coaching is the most appropriate development tool. The human capital consultant (as HR is more optimistically known in PwC) will often be the first point of contact. This avoids the risk of over-enthusiastic or inappropriate use of coaching, or people wanting to pass on their own coaches to others – especially their direct reports. In the early stages, this phase is used as an educative one to ensure the coaching process is handled systematically and professionally. Budgetary issues also need to be resolved at this stage. Coaching is not directly linked to grade although more people at senior levels engage in coaching as a development tool.

The type of issues seen as particularly suited to a coaching approach are:

- Transitions – such as to the role of Partner
- Developing capability
- Dealing with pressure
- Career decisions
- Relationships
- Personal development
- Leadership

The allocation of coaches is determined as a result of conversations with Dee or one of her colleagues at the CCE. Aspects such as learning style and the issues in question are taken into account. There is a certain amount of intuitive decision-making based on a deep knowledge of the available coaches. A coach is found whose knowledge, style and skills would best fit.

Where people wish to go 'offline' and find an external coach, the CCE will help them find or recommend a suitable candidate and ensure boundary issues are resolved.

The internal service has a total of ten coaches who are also involved in a range of other development activities such as action learning and facilitation, which enriches their coaching practice.

Once a coach has been suggested, the client is expected to contact the coach indicating a taking-up of ownership. Depending on the nature of the issue, there may be a three-way meeting with the coach, the client and the sponsor. By starting off in this way, the coach not only is briefed but has the valuable opportunity of observing the relationship between the client and the sponsor. In the majority of occasions, this meeting gives the confirmation that the relationship will work. On rare occasions it does not and the process must be repeated with another coach until the fit is correct.

Contracting is documented. Outcomes are agreed with the sponsor against which success of the coaching will be measured. Often there may be more than one agenda which necessitates a little more rigour initially. Outcomes are usually defined and measured in both quantitative and qualitative ways. This part of the process is relatively new and is awaiting the results of feedback. One aim in this measurement is to make coaching more visible and accountable to the business, without compromising confidentiality. A formal standardised questionnaire using open questions is used at the end of each coaching assignment to assess efficacy. This assesses not only the outcomes of the coaching from a personal perspective, but also seeks the view of the sponsor and looks at the business benefits of the coaching.

There is flexibility in the way that coaching is offered although six sessions seems to be 'the magic number'. Variables such as budget, the demands of time and travel may require more creative approaches such as an intensive few sessions and then further spaced out appointments. Coaching is time bound to avoid the development of dependency.

In the future, Dee envisages a greater use of coaches in time-critical situations, allowing role-playing, video feedback and intensive coaching to achieve a rapid shift in performance. She also seeks to find ways of gaining opportunities to observe and coach clients in real-time situations, such as shadowing in the workplace.

As the rate of change is ever increasing, coaching will be especially relevant for those who need to lead change within PwC. The diversity agenda will drive other applications of coaching. A high degree of energy is being invested in women's development. It is on the board's agenda to increase the number of women at senior levels in the organisation. With this in mind women mentors have been established. Coaching would be seen as a powerful adjunct to that. As a more sophisticated understanding of the value of coaching grows, it is envisaged that if more experienced partners developed their own coaching skills, they could be of even greater value within their own areas.

Another aim is to ensure that coaching becomes or remains linked to organisational development activities, enabling themes to be fed back to the organisation and allowing cross-fertilisation of ideas from the two disciplines.

Although PwC may use predominantly internal coaches there is also a place for external coaches. This may be due to either specialist need, partner preference or pressure on resources. Those on the shortlist of approved coaches will in the first instance happily share PwC's ethics. Credibility, flexibility and negotiated good rates will be other requirements. At present there are 10–15 external coaches. PwC has not gone down the route of employing the larger coaching companies but prefers to deal with individuals where PwC's own internal rigorous quality control can be applied. The existing relationships have developed over time. There has never been a beauty parade initiative and the relationship is demand led. There are no guarantees of work, although there are some programmes where coaching is built in and therefore more predictable. An overall contract is negotiated so that rates are agreed and do not have to be repeated with each new client. External coaches are required to adopt the internal evaluation systems and to collect feedback from their clients. On a quarterly basis, coaches are asked to submit a range of data on clients seen. When possible, all coaches are invited to meet together for exchange of ideas and updates.

Dee, as a psychologist and coach, is keen for a process of regulated standards, such as provided through BPS or BACP for psychologists and counsellors, to be agreed for coaches. Accreditation would ensure rigorous standards and targeted development.

Words of wisdom

Dee's three recommendations for organisations wanting to implement coaching are:

1 Choose your coaches carefully. Important things to take into account are: ethical practice, integrity, willingness to flex and collaborate according to the needs of the organisation, experience.

2 Agree standards for coaching, paths to accessing coaching and a way of evaluating the value of it.
3 Consider coaching alongside other learning interventions so that it can act as a way of enabling greater effectiveness of those interventions, but also so that coaching is not seen as the answer to everything.

Dee's three recommendations for individuals wanting to become coaches in business are:

1 Don't underestimate the sophistication of your buyers – there is nothing worse than being patronised by prospective coaches who assume that the buyer knows little about coaching.
2 Remember that how you come across when you are exploring opportunities is as important as how you come across when you are coaching. The hard sell approach rarely works.
3 A coaching qualification on its own is not enough to guarantee work. Experience, personal style, values and other factors are just as important.

Scottish Power – 'leading from the top'

The company

Scottish Power plc is a £6 billion international energy business listed in London and New York. It provides electricity or gas to 6 million customers in the UK and the USA. It also generates electricity, operates power distribution networks and generally supplies full services to its industry such as metering, billing and call centres. Specialised US businesses extend to coal mining and gas storage.

Coaching at Scottish Power

Four years ago when about to assume the role of chief executive of Scottish Power, Ian Russell sought coaching to prepare and develop in advance of taking over the position. At the time it was a very private arrangement and few in the organisation knew it was happening. Prior to this, coaching had not taken hold in Scottish Power. Previous CEOs had assumed that if you needed coaching you obviously had problems. Following Ian Russell's lead, Sandy Begbie, director of group leadership development and reward, seized the opportunity to legitimise coaching in the organisation at a senior level. In this way, the case for coaching at senior levels was made starting at the very top, expanding to other members of the executive and downwards.

Over 18 months a structured approach to talent management was developed and established. Those considered to be of high potential were identified and coaching was initiated as part of their development. Thus, coaching was presented in this entirely positive light. Coaching had its role to play in the development process as an independent, external and objective voice on career issues which might not be best handled by a line manager. The majority responded with some uncertainty but with open-mindedness and a willingness to try. Success depended on two factors – the quality of the coaches and the operation of a flexible and sensible process.

Scottish Power has stayed away from the larger coaching organisations. Instead they like to buy the individual every time. They prefer to work with a small group of external coaches mainly drawn from single practitioners or from smaller companies. Sandy feels this guarantees a certain loyalty and enduring relationship with the organisation as there is less likelihood of coaches disappearing overnight to different companies. The continuity of the relationship is critical. The sense of ownership on the part of the coach is seen as being more direct in smaller companies. There is otherwise no blanket, standardised profile for Scottish Power coaches. The company has benefited from the fact that Sandy and Colin Duthie – group head, leadership development – have both been in the field for many years, building personal contacts and establishing good relationships with coaches. A critical requirement is that those chosen will have a proven track record and a certain longevity in the field. They will also demonstrate a sense that as a client Scottish Power is very important to them. As Sandy says, 'You know that they always have time for the individuals and for the company.' Coaches will also have a high level of credibility in the eyes of their potential client, largely due to their track record, specialisation and long experience. These factors ensure believability. This is a far more important quality than having themselves been an executive in a company. Price, although a consideration, comes way down the list of relevant factors.

The process for embarking on coaching involves first identifying those individuals deemed high potential and then compiling development plans for each. Coaching at this stage is not mandatory but certain elements are seen as core to success. There is fairly strong pressure to at least explore the benefits of external coaching. Ian Russell continues to be a very keen, active supporter and role model in demonstrating the efficacy of ongoing coaching.

Coaches are really encouraged to understand the workings of the organisation and the talent management process. Sandy recognises that some organisations engage coaches for their personnel quite separately from the working of the business – a 'tick in the box' approach, as he would describe it. In Scottish Power coaches have a good grounding in the business context and the link to the coaching process.

From the preferred list of coaches, attempts are made to match coach and individual. It is here that flexibility is encouraged. It may take several sessions for a coaching relationship to form or it may be that the individual has to meet three or four coaches before the chemistry feels right. Coaching is perceived as a deep and personal process. As such it is essential that individuals feel they are doing the right thing with the right person.

As part of the talent management programme, individuals have an internal mentor from the level above them in the organisation. The mentor, the coach and the client then make for a strong and committed triangle of relationships focusing on development. The mentor ensures that change takes account of the real corporate world while also acting as a champion for the individual who is working to change. Coach and mentor work in tandem in the best interest of the individual.

Major lessons have been learned since the start of this process. It is essential to spend enough time up front to ensure the success of the coaching. A hasty resolution can end up taking longer as it becomes essential to go back and start all over again.

Also, everyone has a very different view of what type of person they can work with. Sometimes there are coaches who do not fit with the expectations of Scottish Power but the individual gets a great deal of benefit from their coaching. They have learned that they need to be careful not to jump to conclusions and to recognise the need to be diverse in their thinking.

In previous organisations Sandy had employed highly sophisticated systems to establish return on investment of similar interventions. He felt that the time and money involved in such a process could not be justified when working at this level with coaching. Evaluation of coaching within Scottish Power comes through regular feedback from those being coached, their line managers and the coaches themselves.

Coaching is seen to have worked very well in Scottish Power. Recognition and acknowledgment from outside is seen as helpful for development as it is more likely to be independent and objective. When wrestling with big issues, those qualities are likely to lead to a better outcome for both the individual and the organisation. Coaching is also seen as an opportunity to address key personal and behavioural issues which would otherwise not be talked about. Coaching effectively prepares people for the next level in the organisation.

In the future, Scottish Power want to do more of the same. Emphasis will be put on improvement of the tracking of specific changes in individuals throughout their career. The coach and the individual will be constantly linked back into the organisation, embedding the process of change. Throughout, Scottish Power has espoused a common-sense pragmatic approach to coaching without any emphasis on developing and monitoring detailed coaching models. This very much reflects the culture of the organisation. Already coaching is extending through the organisation as part of other development programmes such as that for emerging leadership. Further down the organisation, external coaching has less of a part to play as the focus is more on organisation-specific issues.

With regard to the business coaching profession, Sandy feels that although some form of accreditation or regulation is necessary, that will only screen out the really bad, rather than helping to define the really good. Some further classificatory system highlighting the best practitioners would be valuable.

He also feels that HR has a powerful role to play in promoting the role of coaching in developing organisations. Coaches need to impress and work closely with HR professionals to achieve the best through coaching.

Words of wisdom

With all that insight, here are Sandy's tips for businesses introducing coaching and for would be business coaches.

For businesses:

1 If at all possible buy in from the top. The chief executive's open endorsement of the coaching process is very powerful.
2 Embed the coaching process firmly in the company's talent management process.
3 Be flexible and imaginative in choice of coaches rather than clinging to a rigid profile.

And for coaches:

1 Be informed about the company and its business plans and aspirations.
2 Keep communicating with the sponsors.
3 Be clear about your particular strengths as a business coach. Do not dilute this by taking on assignments that are not your forte.

Major Bank – 'flexibility and quality control'

The company

This global commercial bank was, like many of its contemporaries, founded to finance both European wars and reconstruction between them. Today it is a fully integrated commercial and retail bank with about 100,000 staff in 60 countries. It has a very explicit set of values and business principles that all staff are expected to adhere to. At the time of going to press, the bank is going through major changes and has asked for all external descriptions to be anonymised. As the reader will see, this is a powerful case study and we would like to thank the original contributors to the interview.

Coaching at Wholesale Banking

Cathie Stevens is head of leadership and career development of the Wholesale Banking Division: a €6 billion business with 20,000 staff. She joined the bank four years ago. At that point sporadic pockets of coaching were happening. Some knew about it, most did not and others certainly did not understand what it was all about. The traditional approach to training had involved going on courses. There was no preferred supplier list then nor is there now, as such. By 2000 a greater awareness was creeping in largely because people joining the organisation had been exposed to coaching elsewhere and were bringing it with them. However it was not yet being utilised as the powerful development tool which Cathie and her colleagues perceived it to be.

There were variations around the world. In the USA, coaching was already big. The UK and Asia Pacific were a bit behind, except for Australia. Despite the geography, the like-minded were trying to use coaching as a tool. Within her role, Cathie always acted as an internal consultant to answer needs – exploring issues and proposing solutions. More and more she found that her recommendation led to coaching, As time went on, an increasing number of people also started request-ing coaching causing a tremendous change over four years. Initiatives such as a focus on senior management group and team effectiveness gave an opportunity to bring people in to coach around that. This all helped the growth in recognition of coaching as an option in the organisation.

At group level across the whole organisation a programme was developed for very senior people with the purpose of devel-oping their leadership ability. Coaching was offered on a voluntary basis as a part of this. Again, with more of the senior people going through this sort of process and being exposed to coaching, the concepts began to permeate the organisation. Thus, from all these different directions a critical mass of aware-ness was being created. Cathie feels that much of the success of this process is attributable to its organic growth. No one was ever forced into coaching. It was always presented as available to help. Cathie's interviews with people formed a useful test of their readiness to see the value of the process and decide if they wanted it or not. Mostly, however, word of mouth was responsible for the spread of coaching.

The main benefit that Cathie can see for having a greater structure to the process would be the element of quality control. When the group development programme was introduced, with its associated coaching, coaches were required to go through a comprehensive evaluation process before taking part. Previously it had been, and still is, ad hoc. A lot of people still make their own arrangements.

Where it is more standardised, the process leading to coaching usually entails the individual approaching their HR adviser, perhaps Cathie or a colleague. A discussion establishes the level of sponsorship they have in the organisation for the coaching, where the request originated – whether it came from process or concerned a performance issue. Their level of commitment is assessed and addressed before they are given information about how to proceed. As the volume increases, there will be a need to use the internal website more effectively. The aim will be to make available certain information such as what coaching entails, clarifying what they want out of the process, and assurances about confidentiality and security.

After this initial phase the line manager may then enter the equation. If the line manager did not initiate the coaching process then the individual is asked to go back and engage them in the process. Although confidentiality is ensured for discussions within the coaching itself, the process aims to be open and transparent within the organisation. Responsibility, commitment and support are expected of the line manager.

Cathie is very conscious of the need to work at the client's pace, being conscious of their learning readiness, individually and organisationally, rather than trying to push through an initiative because it is deemed right. 'When they're ready to listen, they'll listen,' she says with characteristic pragmatism.

The next phase of the process involves Cathie looking at the possible coaches and selecting two or three she believes might suit. The individual is then asked to contact the coaches directly. This all helps with the process of assessing their commitment to coaching. Once the individual meets and decides on a specific coach then learning objectives are agreed. Who gets involved or informed is decided. The bank does not mandate that the line managers must be involved at this stage but expects consideration of whether they should be. Managers may not need to be active but they probably should be aware of what the objectives are as they form part of the individual's personal development plan.

Cathie sees herself as very much the guardian of quality so is looking for knowledge of objectives, desired outcomes and how well the process has worked for both parties.

Typically the individual will have six coaching sessions, a review part way through and at the end, with consultation and advice about whether further coaching is required. The time scale over which the sessions are conducted is left to the individual and their coach to decide as appropriate to the circumstances. Flexibility is paramount. Styles, as a result, vary dramatically.

One concern is that coaches can become too drawn into the client's agenda and lose sight of the objectives and the organisation's need to profit from the process. It is vital to determine that money is being well spent. If the individual wants to move far from the agreed agenda then the onus is on the coach to address that with the individual. If it is not working then they need to go back and check with the organisation. If the organisation is paying for certain things to be covered, then it is imperative to check that the coaching is on track. By the very nature of the coaching relationship Cathie recognises that many issues will emerge. However, a case would need to be made to the company for a change from agreed objectives.

There is often a tension within coaches regarding the issue of confidentiality which leads to a blanket shutdown of information. Cathie won't use a coach who does not understand and respect the delicate balance needed in protecting the exact content of the coaching sessions but keeping an open and honest dialogue with the company. Similarly, coaches are expected to have an interest in the nature and development of the organisation which forms the backdrop to the coaching contract.

Cathie is very clear in seeing the medium as the message. If coaching is about enabling people to take control over and responsibility for their own development, then any processes around coaching should reflect that aim. Imposing controls to effectively police the process would give a very mixed message.

Nonetheless, there are some things it is still very useful to know:

- The key outcomes have been achieved
- Learning has occurred
- There is observable behavioural change
- Change is embedded and sustainable in daily working life

The organisation, she admits, would probably like more systems tracking exact costs and returns on investment. She also concedes that her approach is probably rather counter-cultural. Her argument for this is that it is only too easy to fit in and do what would be predictable or fit with and perpetuate the existing culture when, in fact, the organisation needs to be challenged to behave in different ways from the traditionally accepted.

So far then, the data regarding the benefits and results of coaching are largely qualitative. Feedback through 360° is used consistently on leadership programmes but otherwise as appropriate. As you might be able to predict by now, Cathie dislikes the idea of being too prescriptive, as she believes not everyone needs this type of feedback. It is just another tool she would employ where appropriate, rather than routinely. Ideally, she admits she would like to have quantitative feedback available to back up the fact that personal experience and all the theories show that it works.

At present at the bank the people being coached are director level upwards, across the organisation and mainly focused on behavioural leadership issues and in transition, such as moving roles. Group coaching is used to help teams look at leadership and behaviours such as communication and trust. This enhances the opportunity to bring the coaching back into the organisation in a proactive fashion.

Although Cathie and her colleagues are capable of coaching, these skills are usually applied to the engagement of people in the coaching process and the commitment to objectives, while the bulk of the coaching is conducted by coaches external to the organisation. In a sense, this is almost a covert way of giving people a chance to experience an early taster of coaching skills. Being a skilled coach herself is also instrumental to being a good judge of external coaches.

With regard to the future, the main focus is on increasing the availability of coaching as a preferred option for the development track. With this in mind, greater focus will be placed on a more structured and strategic use of the intranet site to provide the information which will facilitate self-selection. By providing profiles of coaches and outlines of methodologies, it should relieve some of the pressure on Cathie to provide this first level of information. Focus can then be placed on the all-important clarification and agreement of learning objectives that pay back into the organisation.

The next big issue will be how to capture the knowledge and key themes without taking away from critical confidentiality and trust. It is likely that the bank will want to use more coaches who are prepared to collaborate as teams to pool feedback and insights which have been gleaned from the coaching into the organisation. This will provide return on investment information, which will demonstrate how coaching is benefiting the business and provide themes for change. In this way, the aim will be for coaching to become a systemic, embedded approach which can speed up the change process dramatically.

Another initiative will be to equip all managers with coaching skills as a fundamental set of managerial tools. Not only will this permeate the organisational communication style and development processes, it should also, by giving awareness of the benefits, enhance the openness to external coaching.

With regard to the coaching industry itself, Cathie sees a powerful need for regulation and credentials which in turn will establish it as a serious profession. A system of accreditation such as that now commenced by the Association for Coaching should be an excellent start. She would also like better articulation of the different varieties of coaching and their particular applications. Coaches themselves should aim for greater transparency rather than hiding behind a veil of misplaced confidentiality. They should be very clear about what they do and how they do it. They should be prepared to show their successes and share how they have achieved them, with clear illustration through case studies.

Words of wisdom

Cathie's advice to businesses introducing coaching and to would-be business coaches is, for businesses:

1 Grow coaching organically rather than prescriptively by making it available and desirable rather than obligatory.
2 Ensure the highest levels of commitment by involving line managers in the process.
3 Be prepared to be counter-cultural in order to challenge tradition and encourage innovation through development.

And for coaches:

1 Be conscious of the risk of being diverted too far onto the client's agenda. Do not lose sight of the business objectives.
2 Learn to balance confidentiality and feedback professionally.
3 Be prepared to demonstrate to the organisation the coaching process by which results are achieved. Illustrative case studies would be particularly valuable.

In conclusion: a sophisticated case for coaching

Sponsors have become experienced purchasers and now see coaching as part of their mainstream interventions for senior and sometimes middle management. In their own way they recognise the importance of recruiting, fostering and retaining good people to compete in challenging markets and respect the fact that their people want the best from themselves. They recognise strengths instead of weaknesses and seek to play to these and build on them. They are ready for innovation which is seen as a vital means of speeding up results.

Most of our interviewees are keen to normalise the coaching activity: they want the profession to mature and demonstrate high ethics, clarity about what can be done and sound methodologies and approaches. Coaching should be purchased like other services, and a reasonable level of documentation of interventions and results should be created. The traditional 'big questions' of coaching such as return on investment or confidentiality come as less important than first expected and buyers deal with them pragmatically: coaches must be competent and professional, keep sight of the company's objectives, be priced within market boundaries and document their work. Coaches must also be flexible and be prepared to talk to each other and compare notes in some cases.

Sponsors like to hand-pick coaches and will favour the individual over big brands. They also like to offer their clients a choice between a small number of suppliers. Most will use external coaches, but there is always some kind of internal competence, either as a formal centre of excellence or simply because some of the HR community are trained and willing to help within specific boundaries. Buyers will insist on good business credibility coupled with psychological training or at least safeguards (e.g. supervision, accreditation). They are also quite good at using a coaching approach themselves, letting clients handle their own development, for example.

Ultimately, the mature buyer of coaching is someone who blends this intervention with a number of other developmental approaches to prepare executives for their next level. They want to work regularly with generalists and specialists they can trust and who can become part of the fabric of their services.

How do these good intentions translate in reality? Are clients of coaching feeling supported and developed? Which type of coaching provides merely comfort and which fosters durable change? This is the subject of the next chapter.

Conversations with clients

The previous chapter focused on the wants and needs of the corporation, while this one is dedicated to individual clients. This is about personal stories: one of the main tenets of coaching is the high emphasis on confidentiality; so how do we know exactly what is going on behind closed doors? Five individuals have generously invited us in to understand why they sought coaching, what their reservations were, how they benefited and what advice they would offer. They were willing to be named but we felt it would be more respectful to maintain a degree of confidentiality.

Personal stories

As in the corporate studies in the previous chapter, we have preserved as much of the spontaneity of the interview as possible. Again, we have mixed our clients with those of colleagues so as to get as balanced a view as possible. Our interviewees are:

- Simon – professional services
- John – document management
- Gina – music industry
- David – pharmaceuticals
- Letitia – banking

Simon – 'working effectively with the in-house specialist'

Simon is currently director of business within tax at one of the big four accountancy firms in the UK. He runs a team of 50 people and expects to be a partner within the next year. His role involves him in tax investigations, helping existing clients with serious problems with the Inland Revenue or Customs and Excise. He also manages his team and acts as a consultant adviser on larger FTSE 200 clients. He has to win work, network with tax partners and keep up to date with the technical aspects of his role.

Having studied law at university he joined the Royal Hong Kong Police as an inspector and then became a tax inspector for 11 years. Almost six years ago he was approached by his current firm and became a senior manager working to win business in the UK and consulting with larger clients. He knew the company was committed to development (he had previously not had any development in his career). Having switched from the public to the private sector, he was keen to sharpen his business skills. He was encouraged to manage his career through a formal assessment followed by a senior management development workshop. Having managed to postpone twice he did eventually attend the three-day event. He felt like he had been crucified. Activities included role-playing business situations with professional actors. He turned out to be very goal oriented, brutal and direct rather than consultative. This experience accelerated his decision to have coaching.

Eighteen months he started working with an in-house coach who had a tax background. He considered that a good thing and was reassured by her knowledge and understanding of his subject. He knew she had coached his line manager and she was recommended, all of which helped him make his choice. They entered into an open-ended commitment to coaching, although now he is likely to see her for a lunch or dinner to catch up.

They started by reviewing his life story and noting that however idyllic it had been there were still events that had affected the way he behaved now. They explored the influences and outcomes of these behaviours and perceptions. Simon realised that he tended to do what he perceived to be important rather than taking a longer-term view. She revealed to him what was happening in his life – that his goals in coaching were specifically about relationship-building and how one is perceived. He was unclear about the impact he was having on others. There was always homework. She never took an action point – that was his responsibility. There was relentless scrutiny of his actions and reactions. Simon would try to resist at times but inevitably saw the insights as true. They worked through the outputs of the courses he had done, locking the learning into applications in real life, putting the whole picture together. She helped impose a rigour and a timetable to his aims and achievements. Her approach was analytic and descriptive. Simon was not particularly conscious at the time of what her philosophical or theoretical underpinnings were. The experience was extremely positive.

It gave him the mechanism and framework to continue with development after the formal coaching came to an end. Without that reinforcement, even with great courses being available, learning might not have been applied. Coaching locked in and implemented the development. Translating from theory to practice took into account attitudes and behaviour and above all else made Simon aware of the fact that despite these influences he always had a choice about how to behave.

Simon recognises that coaching contributed to his promotion. He became a better coaching manager of people and winning work that he might not otherwise have won.

Words of wisdom

Simon's advice to those seeking coaching would be:

1 Bad feedback can be good news! Use the opportunity to make effective change through coaching.
2 Make sure that your coach's credentials suit your needs.
3 Do the homework – it locks in the learning.

John – 'from winter to spring in one fell swoop'

As a co-founder and director of a document management company in the City, John first sought coaching because of a recognition of gaps in his skills. At first he was looking specifically at sales and marketing development. Once he embarked on this very focused coaching process, he realised that he might need to engage in more in-depth analysis and broaden the remit. He needed to find out more about his current situation and values and to make an assessment of personal style. Coaching moved him to study more closely his position in the company and his relationship with the other founder. Like many entrepreneurs in new businesses he had worked flat out for years as the company was growing and becoming established. The attitude required had been 'can do, must do, will do'. There was no time to manage anything or anyone. In that position he had become the jack of all trades. Every month was about making sure there was enough business for another month. As a result, he felt he had become a victim of his own success. Despite having completed an MBA just as he set up the company, he lost the ability to manage, finding it quicker and easier to do it all himself. He was so immersed in the minutiae that he could not look strategically at the business any more. Also, his managing director (MD) was a very dominant character and John felt that he was changing from a 'can do' man into a head-down 'yes' man. It was easier not to take the time to debate. Subjugating himself led to a quieter if not happier life.

Pressure had also increased due to external events: getting married, starting a family and the economic impact of September 11 on his City clients all had important personal and business repercussions. Was the business strong enough to survive through the bad times? Relationships became strained at work. He does not feel that he behaved as well as he could have at that time. Things were said that should not have been and derogatory bonuses led to a further reduction in motivation. For a time he felt as if he was operating in a vacuum while still getting on with and worrying about the business.

Coaching for John specifically started when he agreed to be the guinea-pig for a process that would later be extended to all the directors. He found the initial coaching sessions hard as they forced him to face up to tricky issues and thoughts that had been eating away at him and draining any delight out of his role. He felt tired and sorry for himself and at first it was hard to face up to all this out loud with another person. The coaching process began with 360° feedback and psychometrics which made it even more clear that there was no place left to hide. During that period the questions that emerged were, 'What do I want to achieve? What is my future role?' and most specifically, 'Do I want to take over as MD?'

Coaching proved to be a safe environment for getting it all off his chest, saying whatever he wanted in the heat of the moment. It also presented challenges and the need to face topics that had been avoided. There was an opportunity to attempt to understand what was happening, at a deeper level than before. He learned a range of techniques for understanding the motivations and reactions of people in a range of situations. For example, transactional analysis gave a structure to the process of making sense of the impact some of the directors had on each other and gave a blueprint for their future dealings with each other. By assessing his own motivation, John realised that financial gain was not the most significant factor in driving him forward: he was relatively secure, already. It was all about relationships with fellow directors and being able to see the way ahead. Coaching gave peace of mind about the way he and his colleagues could understand each other, develop their relationships constructively, recognise their strengths and weaknesses and establish their value to the company. This enabled the company to move forward in a far more effective way.

John grew to realise that he had a powerful and fitting role to play as vice-chairman, excellent salesman and 'elder states-man'. Although not a person who wants open praise, realising how much respect there was for him was a good feeling. In a sense he had let go and accepted that different skills were now needed for the company to grow. Instead of trying to force himself, or be forced, as a round peg into a very square hole, he had the opportunity to discover his strengths and to play to them. The time had come for the company to move from the entrepreneurial to the professional. It was a real sea change and he allowed himself to admit that he did not want to be the MD who had to make it happen after all. It was up to others to maximise shareholder value through direct action. With this resolution came peace of mind and a two-year plan for moving on to other things.

He describes the change: 'It went from winter to spring in one fell swoop.' The process was hugely cathartic. Critical to this was, John feels, the chance to see himself as a whole being, a total character with values and expectations that had developed through a range of experiences. By aligning his plans with these values he could feel confident that he was making the right moves in his life. His relationship with the other co-founder was revitalised. Because they now knew what triggered conflict, they worked much better together. There was also open and mutual recognition and communication of the invaluable part that John had played in the success and growth of the business. The impact on the rest of the company was palpable.

John feels that the benefits of the coaching were immense and that lessons learned have generalised into other aspects of his personal life and relationships. He finds himself now operating as a sounding board for others, helping them recognise the patterns that emerge and helping them plan appropriate tactics and responses.

Words of wisdom

John is a great advocate for the coaching process and has this advice for those contemplating coaching:

1 Be open minded and prepared to challenge yourself.
2 Don't artificially separate work and home. Be prepared to see the whole person with a range of attributes and talents that can be used across both domains.
3 As there is risk involved through the huge amount of trust you put in the coach, ensure that you are satisfied about how confidentiality will be handled. As much as you would prefer what you say to be safeguarded, sometimes it can be in your best interest for themes to go back to the organisation.
4 It is not all about ranting and getting it out of your system. If things have to be rebuilt to get the results, give it your best shot.

Gina – 'exploring the agenda beyond work'

Gina, HR director in a global music business, was introduced to coaching from two angles at the same time. First, she was investigating various senior team development options following a merger, and met a variety of people involved in coaching. At that point she had not considered looking for coaching herself. Roughly at the same time, she was interviewed for a new job and this provided the second trigger: having flown through the selection process making a great impression at every level, she was to meet the chief executive for final approval. It was a terrible interview. She froze, was flushed, tongue-tied and felt awful coming out of the interview. It was only her second interview in eight years but she realised that the same thing had happened the previous time. Her boss at the time suggested it might be a recurring pattern. He felt she also had some issues with him as an authority figure, something she might need to address.

Because she had already been looking at coaching, Gina felt this issue would be an ideal topic to investigate and work on. She felt very open and confident about the approach: not only did she have a degree in psychology, but she felt comfortable holding her hand up and asking for help. She had already started to do some counselling on intensely personal areas so felt prepared to do something similar in a business context. In reality, as far as the organisation was concerned, she still put the case for the investment in her own coaching to the chairman as an opportunity to pilot interventions for the senior team post merger. Even four years ago she found people were still wary about recognising the value of coaching for development, being more likely to assume an underlying problem. Perhaps, she admits, there was also a little bit of self-protection involved as well.

She had seen quite a lot of coaches who employed a range of processes. What appealed to her about the coach she chose was the structured approach used and the authenticity of the coach. Sessions started with a whole day of self-awareness, using 360° feedback tailored to specific business issues and data from psychometric analysis. This luxury of an intensive process, compared with a normally fractioned business environment, enabled her to get underneath what had been happening in her life. Very quickly, coaching moved into examining the deep personal issues driving her behaviour in one-to-one relationships in the workplace. Being able to stand back and view the broad, panoramic sweep of her life allowed her to get the picture, seeing patterns and making connections for the first time. She describes the depth of personal insight as leading to a truly profound 'aha!' moment of 'Oh my God, I know where this is coming from'. That insight into the origins of her behaviour and how she currently viewed her manager then led to working on how she could begin to change those reactions.

The structure and process used by the coach in shaping the sessions were very important in giving Gina a sense of being in a safe pair of hands. While she could wrestle with realisations and implications, she did not have to worry about where they were going in the coaching process. The coach was in charge of that part, keeping them on track, remaining flexible and never formulaic.

Gina feels it is important for organisations to recognise how often personal circumstances outside work drive behaviour in the workplace. In her own case, she was very confident and competent in her field of expertise and could be forceful and passionate, especially with her peers. It was only when confronted with her own line manager or others in a position of authority that she tended to clam up and stop being true to herself. In those situations her drive was to try to please. In both the interviews, there had been no niceties, no time for getting the other's measure or for bonding. She had no idea where they were coming from and so stumbled over her answers as she did not know how to get them right – what they wanted to hear. Intellectually she knew that her own opinions were as valid as anyone else's, but what dawned on her was that she had always tried very hard to please her mother. This revelation and recognition allowed her to completely change the way she behaved in the workplace.

She still meets up with that old boss and is easily able to be very clear about her own views. By the time she went into the new work relationship – having got the job where she had had the disastrous interview – Gina was very prepared to tell it like she saw it. In a company where there were many toadies currying favour, she was more highly valued because of her tendency to say it straight.

Coaching she believes is very much about relationships. Group training programmes have their place and can lead to some insights, however, where the personal and the business were so closely entwined, she considers it unlikely that she would ever have revealed any of this in a group business setting. In formal training, she might have shared and had a chance to think but only in one-to-one does she believe that she could have got to the root of it all. Vital to coaching is the trust and confidence in the relationship. It is possible to say things there that would not be feasible anywhere else in the business environment. Gina believes there will always be personal issues which will have emerged from previous relationships such as family and school, all prior to the current workplace, which only one-to-one will reveal. Although she feels such issues could also be tackled in counselling, that would lack the essential business focus and an understanding of the realities of the commercial environment. In turn that would have an impact on the effectiveness of the action planning. Business coaches must understand how it feels to be immersed in that type of business environment.

When she moved to her new organisation, Gina discovered that coaching was available for all senior people. They employed a number of coaches. She welcomed this and considered the company enlightened as a result. Coaching there, she soon considered, in fact constituted an abdication of responsibility by the chairman. For him, money was always the answer. By throwing a good deal of funds at coaching, he felt the situation had been dealt with. He did not understand his role in giving respect and recognition. The availability of coaching led to the retention of people for longer than they would otherwise have stayed. However, the coaching itself had become rather unprincipled as two of the coaches used their role as a power play against other people, feeding back confidential information and operating as spies in the organisation.

Her coach however possessed integrity and respected confidentiality, and became an important source of support helping Gina to survive the organisation. The nature of the company was that they only employed the best in their field.

This led to a lot of individual stars but no sense of team whatsoever. This was heightened by the fact that remuneration was based on a review process which ranked each individual against all the others. Bonus was directly calculated from this position. The rankings were established as a result of up to ten 360° reviews. As your peers would be on your review list this produced a dog eat dog mentality, as you contemplated marking them down to ensure you went higher. Individuals all looked out for themselves. Coaching was the only source of support in the whole organisation and allowed for ventilation. This coaching proved very different from the first coaching experience, providing ongoing support for an hour and a half every two weeks. The first coaching sessions had caused an absolute realisation that Gina's life could not be about always pleasing someone else. The other big 'aha!' had been that a working relationship is a two-way process. She had realised that she needed to be able to respect her boss. If she did not, then she would never be comfortable. Gradually Gina came to question whether she was ever going to be happy in corporate life, observing politics and watching people do things she didn't agree with. While she recognised how much she had to bring to an organisation, she began to wonder whether she would need to do it from outside. As her confidence in her skills and opinions grew, she realised that if she could not find respect she would be going against her own values. Gradually she reached the decision to resign. Her health was being affected and there was no room for social life. 'Nothing is worth this,' she thought. She was persuaded to stay by her boss. At that point it became apparent that the business was about to be spun off, they would be made redundant and very large bonuses would be paid. She was wrestling with her conscience, accusing herself of selling out and trying to decide whether she should just go, missing the bonus by two or three months. Sessions with her coach helped her to recognise that she had already worked very hard to achieve this bonus, to which she therefore had a certain entitlement and was no less deserving than the others. She wanted to do other things for which a lump sum would be very useful. She could be honourable but not stupid. She decided to be honest and wrote to her boss explaining the fact that she wanted to go but laying out how she could add value in the meantime. She was explicit but her boss still found it unthinkable that she would actually go. When the time came she felt confident that she had been very clear about her intention but her boss still behaved quite badly, seeing himself as rejected by her. He was petulant, making her serve her notice but excluding her from meetings. Gina, in contrast, was confident that her behaviour was professional. She understood that he was going through a version of a grief process from denial to anger through to acceptance. She waited and recognised each stage without becoming upset. Because of her preparation, she carried on being professional, using her knowledge of him to predict his behaviour rather than hoping he would behave differently.

Having recognised her desire to work outside organisations, Gina decided to take stock and enjoyed the best part of a year out. She then set up her own HR consultancy and honed her coaching skills. She now feels she has a very balanced life, which is both more rounded and fulfilling.

Words of wisdom

Coaching had a profound part to play in initiating Gina's self-awareness and change. Her advice is:

1 Go and try the experience – those most senior, who think they do not need it, often need it most of all.
2 Be open in the process.
3 Make sure that you are truly contemplating coaching for yourself. If coerced it is unlikely to work.
4 Recognise that events in your personal life can have a major impact on your performance in your working life.

David – 'catching up with his experience'

A science manager in a world-class academic research institution, David was seeking an alternative career path. He felt he was in a rut in his current job and could see no way of matters improving. He had no idea about how to go about the process of change and was floundering. Trawling the web looking for inspiration he stumbled by accident across an interesting site which asked, 'If you think you are interested, why not ask someone?' He clicked to do so. It didn't work and so he phoned to tell them this. There ensued a conversation by the end of which he had a recommendation for a coach. When he called, in true coaching fashion, the coach asked, 'What makes you think that coaching would be of interest?' Immediately he was forced into thinking hard about his situation. The conversation developed and they decided it would be worth getting together informally to explore his motivation for looking for assistance at this time. It felt like stepping into the unknown.

With many reservations, David turned up and was surprised that the conversation did not immediately hone in on specific jobs but started to make him find other ways of looking at his skill set. He had little confidence about exploiting his knowledge base into another arena. Scientifically trained, he felt his expertise was very narrow in definition. The coach made him look at the other life skills he had acquired.

David recognised that this process would give him the opportunity to 'think outside the box' and so they agreed to meet regularly on a more formal basis. David embarked on a total of six sessions over three months.

His scientific background had given him tremendous focus but had also made him blinkered and very negative in his perspective when he asked himself the question, 'What do I have to sell to anyone?' He had no sense of the direction in which to pursue his job search and so could not move forward. At first he found coaching quite a daunting prospect and was unsure of the outcome. While he recognised that it was a worthwhile exercise, it still required a leap of faith. There was an element of risk involved, namely that he might find out things about himself that he would not like. He admits he had been driving his wife up the wall talking about the situation at home. He had had nowhere else to take it but saw how hard it was for a partner to be totally impartial and objective. Coaching allowed him to explore the issues without overburdening his long-suffering wife. He could bring enthusiasm back home while dealing with life-changing decisions. Also there was no need to be concerned about the coach's feelings, which was also a relief.

One of the first discussion points concerned what made David tick and when he was at his most perky so that he could think about and plan to do difficult things at the most effective time. He found it useful to learn about some of the subtleties of human behaviour and to be given the statistics about aspects of his search (e.g. the small percentage who get new jobs through applications compared to those who achieve a change through networking). This was powerful and encouraged him to contact people in ways he would never previously have considered. He found that this kept him motivated and focused. In two months, of all the people he approached, only one person refused to see him and most were very helpful. Having to implement new behaviours worked on breaking down old beliefs where the statistics alone would not have been enough. It showed him not to write things off. The coach also asked David to consider all the jobs that surrounded him – waiter, bookseller, dustman, and asked him to consider whether he could see himself in that job. This helped develop clarity about what he could and could not see himself doing. Over two or three meetings, his thinking changed from an unfocused to a more logical style. He used his own scientific ability to test various hypotheses. He recognised that he had previously been following a tightly-defined career path without looking long term. Building a picture of his skill set enabled him to look wider.

The previous uncertainty had knocked his confidence. Although at times it was unpleasant to be prodded out of his comfort zone, it did much to rebuild his confidence. At the time, David was not sure that he recognised how much value he got out of the coaching process – after all, he was paying for it himself. Only later, on reflection, did he appreciate what it had done for him. He has been left with a lasting imprint. He no longer has a head-down attitude. He is much more likely to be scanning possibilities and asking himself, 'Where would I fancy going next?' He keeps his options open and does not feel locked in any more. Coaching forced him to think more laterally and look at the big picture. He now knows what he values, in terms of a career instead of solely what he was trained to do. He acquired tools and a process to go down a new path (e.g. networking). Recognising that he had innumerable skills, even though he didn't have certificates to prove it, raised his confidence and made the whole process easier and attainable.

Within the space of a few months, he knew exactly what he had to do and was happy to get on with it. He is now leading scientific teams for one of the world's largest drug companies. High value had been generated in a very short time. He is much more positive, motivated and confident. Coaching had made him look at the world differently. Dispelling the myth he had invented about the narrowness of his range of skills caused no less than a paradigm shift in his thinking. David believes that the coaching, while not specifically getting him the job he is currently in, strengthened him and started him on a steep learning curve. Some say that denial of the coach's intervention is the ultimate compliment an egoless facilitator can receive . . .

Words of wisdom

Coaching for David was, as he says, a life-changing experience but he cautions that you must be prepared to trust a process which can seem at first quite alien. His advice to those considering coaching is:

1 If you feel anxious about embarking on the coaching process, test it out with a first session before committing yourself.
2 Then, take a leap of faith to overcome residual doubts.
3 One of the best things is to have your tunnel vision about your capabilities challenged so you can see the big picture.

Letitia – 'becoming a political animal'

Letitia is the head of sales for Europe Middle East and Africa (EMEA) and an executive director of a large bank. When she was promoted to this prestigious position, she was very conscious that such a move was traditionally a case of sinking or swimming: companies usually provide no support. This is not necessary by design: people don't ask for help because they are very conscious of the risk of being perceived as weak. She felt her own weakness was an incapacity to 'do the politics' which might be required in her new role. Instead of playing a clever game, she felt at risk of holding back, keeping a tight rein on her emotions which would then escape inappropriately at times. As a result she felt she failed to come across as professional and coolly rational.

Her previous boss came from a different part of the bank. He had asked for coaching when he took up his new position. He also arranged a team-building event for the whole team. After the first day, the niceties had been stripped away, revealing everything that was wrong. Letitia described it as open-heart surgery with pints of blood lost. Initially, she just could not see how it could all be put back together again. Yet it was over in the next few days, with a productive impact on development.

She knew that her boss was politically astute – he did not show his emotions and could read the signs very well in the organisation. So, if he thought that it was acceptable to ask for a coach and get one, she resolved that she would do the same. The case she made for coaching was that:

- She had not been responsible for as big a role before.
- She would have wider contacts within the bank than previously
- It would be good for the business.

Only then did she discover how many people already had coaches. Some even had two – one to deal with their lack of interpersonal skills and the other to focus more closely on direct business goals. HR recommended a coach to her. They had a first session to determine whether she was comfortable with his style. Letitia tends to be instinctive and intuitive so knew at once that she could talk openly and honestly with total trust. She was conscious of his empathy right away and felt very comfortable. Her initial contract was for six sessions which, by necessity of travelling, had to be quite spaced out over a year.

Initially, they set out their stall. Letitia shared why she wanted coaching and what she wanted to achieve. The coach set out how he wanted to run their meetings, establishing a framework to check how they were doing or whether they needed to make adjustments. Early on, Letitia was encouraged to set up a 'board of directors' – i.e. a range of people who could help her succeed and position herself. One clear goal was to develop these wider relations.

Previous development experiences had left Letitia striving to be other things that the organisation seemed to want. Coaching by contrast gave her an opportunity to acknowledge and celebrate who and what she was and to be proud of her attributes. She feels that many people in companies are aspiring to be things they are not and as a result attempt to mould them-selves, gradually becoming twisted out of shape. The analogy she used was one of wearing ill-fitting shoes – a painful process which gradually distorts your feet until you become so used to the discomfort that it seems normal. Not all people want to keep going up through the organisation in a methodical fashion, yet there is little reward or recognition for those courageous enough to decide they want to go another route.

Letitia had never been clear at school about what she wanted to do – everyone seemed to assume that you must know what you want. As a result she found her way into a bank for a summer job and decided to stay, studying for a banking diploma. The benefit of working for an international bank, she has discovered, is that there is a wide range of varied oppor-tunities. She had always worked in financial services but through coaching came to recognise that her key strengths lay in dealing effectively with people. Her management style she discovered was effectively a coaching one. By recognising where her strengths lay she then had to face the implications about where her future career should lie. She found it was worth the investment to move out of her comfort zone.

Much of the coaching focused on developing professional rather than personal relationships. Carefully planning her encounters, Letitia concentrated on approaching senior people, having something useful to say and communicating that effec-tively. Her coach also helped her become aware of the occasions when others found her threatening and also of those people for whom she could not find answers. This enabled her to let her-self off the hook, recognising that the problem might lie in the other person rather than herself. She worked on consciously recognising her emotions and making choices about her actions and the impact they would have. She realised how much emotions could get in the way of the desired results if she did not channel them well.

Having always felt the need to contribute to demonstrate that she had earned her place, Letitia learned to listen more, to sit calmly with a more senior group, two stages further up the organisation than herself. She asked more questions rather than attempting to make especially apposite or impressive statements. She realised that the way she labelled communication had changed. Previously disparaging about 'political' behaviour, of which she felt herself incapable, she came to see the positive side of planned professional communication while still eschewing negative, manipulative, destructive behaviour. This produced a good fit with her personal values.

By the end of the first six sessions, Letitia felt they had achieved a great deal but not everything she would like to and signed on for another six. The first phase of coaching had dealt mainly with relationships with those above her in the bank. The second phase concentrated more on the team. There were a number of challenges to manage but coaching had already taught her the benefit of getting the other person to look into the mirror themselves to check whether perception might be distorted. Asking the other person questions opened issues up. As a result, appraisals became highly effective in producing positive development. She still has some concerns about putting everything back together again, what to do with the information that you get and how to package the message and move the other on.

One great aspect of her working relationship with her coach was the opportunity to ring up between sessions and discuss real situations as they were about to be played out. Running things aloud past a trusted adviser was invaluable.

Letitia would say that the best outcomes of coaching for her were:

- Acknowledging she felt good about herself and her true strengths.
- Identifying and crystallising what she should be doing with her life.
- Recognising that her facilitative style of management is effective, even though different from other unit managers' more aggressive styles.
- Being able to control her display of emotion, including at times deliberate and appropriate use of controlled passion.

Letitia feels that companies have an amazing source of talent in their people which often goes untapped until people leave or are got rid of. Starting from a talent and strengths perspective she recognises that companies could harness a great deal more motivation than they do presently. With regards to the future, Letitia has discovered that her real strengths lie in the managing of people using a coaching approach to get the best out of them. She feels it would give the bank a great opportunity to use her talent – she knows banking.

Words of wisdom

Letitia's advice to anyone considering coaching is:

1 If you are offered coaching take it. You will find out something really good about yourself.
2 Keep an open mind.
3 Observe the health warning – this may change your life, for good. There will be change and turmoil leading to self-fulfilment but no going back.

In conclusion

These examples show that business people will seek coaching for very different reasons, but there are some universal themes: all were at a stage of intense personal questioning somehow related to self-perception, competence and relationship with others. It would have been easy to take a counselling approach and to 'find and cure a problem'. Instead the coaches used a wide range of skills and evidence to liberate their clients from constraining behaviours, perceptions and emotions and set them free to reach the next level in their career. Those who were not already in transition by and large stayed in their business and made an impact on their relationship with others, often becoming staff coaches themselves and basically more mature managers.

It is interesting to note that most successful business people are intensely curious and occasional intense self-questioning is a near-universal experience, even when not explicit. To quote Gina: 'those most senior, who think they do not need it, often need it most of all'. We also know that clients cannot be forced into coaching. So the most important role for HR professionals may well be to institutionalise coaching as a regular developmental step.

All clients benefited tremendously from the experience, but the process was not always pleasant, particularly at the beginning. The coach's use of objective data coupled with a supportive yet neutral attitude helped tremendously. Some of the discomfort came from the realisation that work and life could not be separated that easily and that they had to investigate the causes of emotions and behaviour beyond the relatively secure four walls of the business. This raises the questions of positioning of the coaching intervention, confidentiality, agenda boundaries and limits of competence for the coach. These are the subject of the next chapter.

Professional issues in business coaching and their solutions

Throughout this book we have signposted best practice, the need to have a clear view and robust processes to deal with contracting (with both client and sponsor), issues concerning confidentiality, the need for supervision and the relationship with various professional bodies. We have also indicated that there were cases which should be referred to other professionals who are more versed in psychology or business than the contracted coach.

The aim of this chapter is to alert readers to the professional factors involved in coaching as well as some of the dilemmas and challenges, and also to propose practical solutions. We cover the following subjects:

- Contracting
- Confidentiality
- Professional bodies
- Professional development
- Diversity
- Supervision
- Boundaries
- Referring clients

Contracting

There are a number of professional issues that need to be taken into account when undertaking business coaching and perhaps the most important is that of contracting. When working in a personal coaching context, contracting is usually straightforward: it simply means agreeing and being clear about the terms and conditions, personal/professional goals, feedback structures and outcome measures to be used (West and Milan 2001). Business coaching contracting needs to reflect the additional dimension of the needs of the organisation (Caplan 2003). Usually, the organisation is paying for the coaching and so, not surprisingly, will want to know that it gets value for money and that the coaching will add to the productivity of the employee and will benefit the health and profitability of the company. A coach is likely to be approached by the line manager, an HR specialist or, alternatively, by those who have sufficient autonomy and authority to organise their own coaching. In such situations the coach needs to be clear not only about the terms and conditions of the coaching but also about the outcomes being sought by each party.

Contracting should cover the following areas:

- Terms and conditions and information pack
- The behavioural contract

Appendix 1 contains examples of forms and contracts allowing us to focus on the rationale for and process of contracting in this section.

Terms and conditions and information pack

It is helpful to have written terms and conditions that can cover all the administrative and professional details that remain common to all organisations. By taking the trouble to think through such issues before starting work with the client you minimise the probability of misunderstandings later on in the coaching process. The information for this can be provided in the form of an information sheet and the headings that would need to be considered include:

- *Aim of the coaching contract* – an outline of the three-way nature of the coaching relationship and the terminology used (e.g. corporate client, coach and designated client).
- *Coaching objectives* – how the process will work. For example, 'at the outset, the coach will take a brief from both the corporate client (e.g. the line manager to whom the individual reports and/or from HR) and from the designated client. These discussions form the basis for the initial objective-setting for the coaching together with mechanisms to be used to measure outcome and will be confirmed in writing'.
- *Conflict resolution* – how disagreements or dissatisfaction with the coaching process will be addressed.
- *Confidentiality and feedback* – a clear statement about confidentiality, its importance, what it means in practice and the process for feedback. In addition, information about duty of care and the fact that feedback to the corporate client by the coach will be discussed with the client in advance needs to be made explicit.
- *Pricing* – information regarding length of sessions and fee costs including factors that could influence additional costs (e.g. use of psychometrics).
- *Location and frequency* – details regarding location and frequency of sessions.
- *Cancellation policy* – all factors pertinent to cancellations (e.g. the cancellation notice period and amount of fee payable).
- *Conflict of interest* – what action should be taken if such a situation occurs? This statement is probably of more use to those who work as associates than for coaches working independently.
- *Professional issues* – here information on aspects such as supervision, continuing professional development (CPD), membership of professional bodies and mention of the ethical framework applied is useful.

In addition to the terms and conditions it may also be useful to produce a brief information pack about who you are, how you work and what you do, together with the names of corporate sponsors with whom you have worked. This is perhaps more of a personal PR/branding item but is worth considering when designing your coaching materials.

The behavioural contract

A contract is, well, just a contract. If coaching is going to produce durable and positive change, it needs to be expressed in behavioural terms.

Some coaches have embraced the concept of a behavioural contract as described by Skiffington and Zeus (2003). Its objective is to ensure that all parties agree the desired outcome from the outset, in behavioural terms. It helps clients and sponsors to get a better feel for what will actually happen behind closed doors and to form expectations about change. The more transparent this part of the process the less likely the disappointment for the corporate sponsor and client. In addition, this also means that there is less chance of the coach being used as a scapegoat if there are political challenges in the organisation.

Setting the scene

In an ideal world the coach, the corporate sponsor and the client would have a joint meeting to discuss the desired outcome. However, this is not always possible; the example below shows how separate discussions can be written up and then signed for so that the contract becomes effective. The behavioural contract will be drawn up as part of the coach's chosen framework: it doesn't dictate how coaching should take place, it simply makes outcomes specific.

Here is a typical introduction to the meeting (involving the sponsor and the client):

> *Thank you for agreeing to meet me to clarify what you would both like to achieve from the coaching process. By the end of this meeting we will have agreed the overall outcomes as well as the specific outcome measurements to be used to evaluate the success of the coaching programme.*
>
> *I have brought along a copy of the behavioural contract that we will be working to and, once we have agreed the outcomes, I shall take this away to be typed and will then send a copy to each of you for signature.*

Coaching objectives and outcome measurement

The next part of the process is to set overall objectives. The coach starts by asking each individual what he or she wants from the coaching process. Coaching skills are important at this stage, as there may be a need to mediate and facilitate the discussion quite proactively. It is frequent for example that a direct sponsor (e.g. line manager) has a fairly narrow view of the scope. The coach will typically start with an open question such as, 'What outcomes do you wish to see from the coaching process?' and then takes it in turns to discuss each aspect with both parties in a bid to gain agreement.

A coaching objective may be a more general statement, such as:

- 'I would like to be more confident.'
- 'I think James and his colleagues would benefit if he could communicate more effectively.'
- 'I would like to feel more in control of what happens.'

This part of the discussion helps the coach to gain information such as an overall perspective of the client, his or her situation, the culture of the organisation, the type of people the client works with, the situations he or she has to face and how he or she is perceived.

Outcome measurement

This is where the discussion starts to get really interesting. The coach needs to help translate objectives into expected new behaviours, as in the following examples:

- 'You said you would like James to communicate more effectively with his team. What would you notice happening if he were being a more effective communicator?'
- 'How would you know if you were more in control of what you were doing?'
- 'What would others be seeing that would be different if you were more in control?'

It is important to get clearly identifiable outcomes as 'communicate more effectively' could mean anything from being more assertive when chairing meetings to briefing staff members on a regular basis or ensuring that systems are in place to impart information (e.g. group e-mails, weekly e-mailed update etc.). All of these can be measured and it is here that those coaches used to the SMART goal-setting model will see similarities. A behavioural model aims to turn all objectives into measurable outcomes. For some coaches not used to this way of working the task can seem rather daunting. However, there is very little if anything that cannot be made concrete. Even the most emotional of desires such as 'I want to feel happy' can be turned into something measurable with simple questions like, 'If you were happy what would you be doing, feeling or thinking that is different to now?'

Obviously, some information may come up later in the coaching process that has an impact on the overall outcome. Nothing is perfect and there may be occasions where the contract may need to be modified at a later date. However, if this were the case then the coach would need to ensure all parties found it acceptable. Alternatively, it is more likely that any changes will be in addition to rather than in place of what has been agreed.

Confidentiality and feedback

The dilemma when undertaking coaching in organisations is the need for such organisations to have some form of feedback and the need for confidentiality to be maintained with the client. During the contracting process it is important for all parties to agree the feedback and confidentiality agreement. An example of such clauses as well as all other elements of the behavioural contract are in Appendix 1.

Summary

A behavioural contract allows all parties to be clear about expectations and delivery. Its strengths are in its clarity and some would say that its weakness is in its concreteness. We suspect that those who find behavioural contracting a challenge may do so more due to a lack of practice than through any fault of the process itself.

Some may argue that a client is unlikely to be explicit about all their objectives at the first meeting, especially in front of the sponsor. We believe that this contract has an important role to play in setting boundaries: we have seen too many coaches being used as emotional blankets with organisations getting very little in return for their investment. The contract provides a minimum level of results. All will be even happier if more can be achieved.

Confidentiality

Confidentiality in the coaching relationship is seen as being of paramount importance to the success of the process. In a one-to-one personal or life coaching relationship, confidentiality relates only to the agreement made between the coach and the client and needs only to take into account generic legal obligations. However, in a business coaching context the sponsoring organisation becomes a third party and the coaching client is likely to be concerned about the issue of confidentiality in relation to the information that the organisation will be privy to (Peltier 2001). Therefore, it is essential that the coach, client and sponsor are clear about what confidentiality means.

Under UK law no one, apart from a lawyer, is able to offer the prospect of total confidentiality to anyone. The legal reality is that a practitioner can refuse to answer questions or turn over documentation if asked to do so by any third party, including the police. However, if issued with a subpoena or court order then the practitioner has little choice but to hand over all materials or face being charged with contempt of court and/or having the material forcibly taken. The only exception to this rule is where Customs and Excise or issues relating to national security/anti-terrorism are concerned. In such cases all materials can be instantly seized.

In reality the issue of confidentiality is less of a problem than it may first appear. When working with organisations it is best, as in the behavioural contracting process above, to be clear at the outset as to what confidentiality means. It is quite a common practice to agree the goals and feedback structure with the client and sponsoring organisation but to make clear to both parties that whatever is talked about in the coaching sessions remains confidential. For example, an agreed outcome known to all parties may be 'to improve the ability to be assertive in meetings by using a range of identifiable assertiveness techniques'. However, when the coach and the client start to work together the client may disclose that he or she has always had problems being assertive and how these issues have a more personal aspect to them. Here any subsequent feedback will be around the practicalities of the techniques being used rather than disclosure of personal issues. In other words, the sponsoring organisation needs to know about outcome but not process.

It is also important to ensure that the laws of the land are adhered to and 'duty of care' is an important issue. If a client were to disclose intent to do physical harm to another, or had carried out such an act, then the coach would need to have made it clear that he or she would automatically disclose such matters to the relevant authorities. These are extreme cases and ones where given that coaching is about dealing with a non-clinical population (i.e. working with people who do not have mental health issues) such comments would be seen as quite normal.

In addition, if there are any special provisos that the organisation wishes to impose, these can be discussed at the outset. For example, a number of organisations such as those in the transport business have stringent rules about safety and if it were to come to light that a train driver or airline pilot had an alcohol problem then disclosure would be seen as essential and would be built in as an exception to the confidentiality agreement. The important thing is that *all* parties are clear from the outset.

From time to time there will be those within sponsoring organisations that want more information than has been formally agreed. In such cases, the coach needs to explain clearly that, while they would like to assist, the information required would break the original confidentiality agreement. This is one of those dilemmas that there is no way around and has to be tackled openly, honestly and within the original parameters of the coaching contract.

Professional bodies

There is no statutory regulation of coaches in the UK at the moment and, given the complications faced by the therapeutic community, it is unlikely that such regulation will take place for at least the next five years. There are advocates for and against statutory regulation. Some people believe it is the only way to go as a way of providing public protection, while others believe that all such regulation will do is hamper the creativity of coaches and have no impact on public safety. No doubt the debate will continue for some years to come if the experiences of other professions are anything to go by. For example, almost a century on, management consultants are still unregulated.

However, like most professions or industries, the coaching world has now developed to the extent that it requires a professional body to consider issues such as standards, ethics and good practice as well as providing a focus for coaches themselves. At the moment there are a range of professional bodies in the UK representing the coaching world (Jarvis 2004). The following information is correct at the time of writing but may change.

The ICF

The oldest professional association is the International Coach Federation (ICF). It was founded in the USA and came to the UK some nine years ago. It has a code of ethics and complaints procedure, provides standards, runs an accreditation scheme, runs conferences and continuing professional development workshops. It has approximately 600 UK members and provides a register of coaches. In 2004 the ICF defined itself as follows: *'The International Coach Federation is the professional association of personal and business coaches that seeks to preserve the integrity of coaching around the globe'*. The ICF UK can be reached via www.coachfederation.org.uk.

The Association for Coaching (AC)

Founded in 2002, this is already the largest UK-based professional association. It has interest groups covering all aspects of coaching, from executive/business to life/personal, specialty and group coaching. The Association has a code of ethics, a code of conduct and provides individual coach accreditation. It also sets coaching standards and operates a complaints procedure in its aim to raise the professionalism and quality of coaching. It carries out and publishes research, organises conferences and continual professional development events. There are currently some 700 members (profiled online) and a further 1000 interested parties. It defines itself as follows: *'The Association for Coaching is an independent non-profit organisation with the goal to promote best practice, raise awareness and standards across the coaching industry, while providing value added benefits to its members – whether they are professional coaches or organisations involved in coaching'*. The Association can be reached via www.associationforcoaching.com.

The European Mentoring & Coaching Council (EMCC)

This international organisation was founded in October 2002 and sees itself as *'An inclusive body covering a broad spectrum of organisations from the voluntary and community, professional training and development, life coaching and academic psychology sectors'*. The EMCC includes mentoring in its remit and has approximately 70 per cent individual and 30 per cent corporate members. There is a complaints procedure and a code of ethics. The EMCC sets coaching standards and provides conferences, continual professional development and supervision. The EMCC can be reached via www.emccouncil.org.uk.

The Coaching Psychology Forum (CPF)

This specialist group was founded in September 2002 and sees itself as *'Promoting the academic and professional development of coaching psychology, and encouraging its research and study in a variety of personal, organisational and training contexts'*. Membership is restricted to those who are psychologists and members of the British Psychological Society. The forum offers a code of ethics, a complaints procedure and code of conduct. It provides conferences, continual professional development, an online register of members and articles on coaching. The CPF can be reached via www.coachingpsychologyforum.org.uk.

Why belong to a professional body?

From a purely pragmatic point of view it is certainly in the interests of an individual coach to belong to a professional body. When a coach becomes a member he or she gains access to a wealth of knowledge and useful networks, and attracts credibility in the eyes of the world. As purchasers of coaching become more sophisticated, many ask whether an individual has any affiliation with a professional association.

Some concern has been expressed about the number or coaching bodies in operation. Certainly there does appear to be an overlap in some of the services offered. However, at this stage in the development of coaching in the UK, diversity of choice is something that adds to rather than detracts from the development of coaching. Perhaps a confederation or consortium approach may develop as this has worked well in other industries.

Professional development

Continued, continuing or continual professional development (CPD) is commonplace in many professions. For example, solicitors, accountants, counsellors and psychotherapists are all required to undertake a certain number of hours of CPD per year to ensure an individual's skills and knowledge are kept up to date. In the therapeutic arena an individual can lose his or her accreditation as a practitioner if there is a failure to undertake the required number of hours.

The coaching world is also engaged in CPD and bodies such as the Association for Coaching require members to undertake 30 hours of CPD per annum. Activities that go towards CPD include attending training courses, seminars and conferences, reading coaching books, writing on coaching-related matters and providing coaching training. CPD is divided into 15 hours of input (i.e. those activities that the coach attends as a student or delegate) and 15 hours of output (i.e. those activities where a coach may be running a course or writing an article). Most coaches find themselves undertaking more than the 30 hours a year once they sit down and work out all the activities they are involved in. The Association for Coaching has a specially designed CPD form on its website (www.association forcoaching.com) which individuals can download for their own use.

It is likely that, as the coaching world progresses, all professional bodies will make CPD a mandatory activity.

Diversity

Coaching takes place in a variety of settings and with a range of individuals from diverse backgrounds. Diversity covers not just race, religion, gender and sexuality but also organisational culture (Spencer 2004). A coach needs to develop a cultural awareness of the clients that he or she is likely to work with and the kind of social, political and environmental factors that are likely to affect them.

Business coaching in Europe can be particularly tricky, because companies are made up of many nationalities and work experiences. Business school or company culture may in fact have a homogenising effect. A coach should make no assumptions but simply keep a look out for differences. For example, a coach may be called in to work on communication issues with a team of people. The team may comprise a Swedish director (male), a German deputy (male), two Americans (both female), three British (two male and one female) and one Asian (male) members of staff. The company may be based in the UK but be a part of a global operation. In such a situation not only does the coach need some understanding of the cultural variations and norms of each individual but also an understanding of the company culture and the international perspective. Nancy Adler (2001) from McGill University is probably the academic who has written most on the subject of cross-cultural management and the role of women in international management.

At its most basic language is the biggest cultural barrier. Forget the jokes about 'separated by a common language', clients feel and behave differently when they are expressing themselves in different languages. It is important that the coach works at the linguistic root level when dealing with emotions and thought patterns. An easy way is obviously to align coach and client along nationality or at least language. Many clients insist on 'native only' coaching for example. This feels instinctively right, but sponsors should be wary of possible 'cultural collusion' between client and coach.

It is not always possible to provide full language matching, especially for large multinational companies. We have found that a practical approach that works well is to offer coaching materials and psychometrics in the mother tongue of their client, even if coaching meetings take place in English.

Supervision

Supervision is a concept largely inherited from psychotherapy and related disciplines. In the context of business coaching what is supervision and should coaches be supervised – and if yes, how?

Definitions

Supervision is the term used to describe the relationship between a coach who makes a formal arrangement to meet with a more experienced coach to discuss his or her coaching work. Supervision provides the individual coach with a place to debrief, to share challenges, to analyse success and to develop his or her abilities. Perhaps the word itself is an unfortunate one as it may suggest a controlling relationship when good supervision is in fact an enabling process.

Proctor and Inskipp (1988) stated that the aim of supervision was to:

- Consider responsibility for standards and ethics.
- Share the responsibility for the professional development of the supervisee's skills, knowledge and understanding.
- Provide opportunities for the discharge and recharging of batteries.

Certainly, those coaches who are also professionals in other helping arenas such as psychology, counselling and psychotherapy are used to the supervisory process and see supervision as being part of good practice.

Michael Carroll (1996) states that there are five tasks in supervision:

1 *Setting up a learning experience* – this includes negotiating a contract with the coach.
2 *The teaching task of supervision* – this includes considering the way the coach learns best and applying differing teaching methodologies such as direct information giving and experiential learning in the session.
3 *The supportive task of supervision.*
4 *The consulting task* – this includes discussion of coaching work, the way in which the coach and client relate to one another and also the relationship with the supervisor.
5 *The evaluation task* – includes consideration of the range of ways in which the coach can monitor and evaluate their work.

The coaching supervisor helps the coach to develop his or her theoretical understanding and skills, to develop a coherent coaching philosophy and to explore additional/further training needs and additional areas of professional development. Supervision is also a key mechanism to address boundary and referral issues, detailed below.

Is supervision necessary?

Coaching supervision is seen by some as a professional necessity and by others as something that coaches can choose to use if they so desire but not something that needs to be made mandatory. We think that there are two ways to look at this question: from an ethical point of view and from a commercial one.

Ethically, we are convinced that some form of supervision is necessary, although it may not have to be formalised, as in psychotherapy. The reason for this is that business coaching is full of grey areas and coaches seldom have the luxury of a very long relationship during which they can address all of their client's issues. It is therefore important to prioritise and to discuss with a neutral sounding-board what interventions are likely to be the most effective in a business context. An interesting side issue is that the supervisor must be bound by the same pledge of business confidentiality as the coach, if only to satisfy stock market regulators. This is why coaching supervision is often internal to a company.

Commercially, we observe a wide variation in requirements. In Chapter 5 for example we saw that PwC had very strict guidelines regarding supervision. These are usually driven by the background of the sponsor: if the HR directors are qualified psychologists, they will usually demand proof of some form of supervision. As a result, business coaches should be prepared to demonstrate that supervisory arrangements are in place, even if only as a proof of quality control. The response of coaching companies obviously tracks client requirements. For instance, many organisations which use associate coaches often offer supervision internally and others ask for the coaches they use to have an external supervisor.

Boundaries

It is important that the coach has a clear personal understanding of the differences between coaching and counselling (William and Davis 2002). In some ways the basic skills of coaching are also the basic skills of counselling. Listening and communication skills used by both activities come originally from what were called 'basic counselling skills' and comprise techniques such as creating an enabling relationship (e.g. the skills of empathy, respect and genuineness), and communication skills such as paraphrasing, summarising, using open questions and challenging. Although the tools are the same at this basic level there are, of course, key differences between the activities. We refer the reader back to Chapter 2 for a review of Egan's helping model of counselling.

Coaching training makes a point of helping students consider the differences between the two and, more importantly, when to refer a client on for counselling. As there are now many psychologists, counsellors and psychotherapists who are entering the coaching industry it is equally important that such individuals understand the boundaries and differences between the activities.

A simple way of thinking about the differences is to use the plus and minus model. If you consider zero as the mid and neutral point, then in counselling a person would start from a minus position, depending on the degree of emotional distress experienced, and the aim of the work would be to help the individual recover by moving back to zero. In coaching the client would start from a zero position and be seeking to move to a plus position. In other words, counselling relates to an individual's mental and emotional health while coaching is seen as a form of personal development.

There are many definitions of what counselling and psychotherapy entail. For the purpose of this section we will distinguish between two clinical interventions: straightforward counselling which involves dealing with emotional distress, and psychotherapy where something is 'damaged' inside. The latter tends to involve changing the person at an intrinsic core level and can last as long as two to five years. But what does this mean in a business context and how does this compare to coaching? Consider the following example:

Julie has just been newly-appointed as an account executive for a well-known public relations consultancy. She is delighted as this is her dream job. However, she is concerned that while she builds excellent relationships on a one-to-one basis with her clients she flounders when it comes to group presentations and she is now expected to make presentations to clients and is worried that she will not be able to work effectively.

Coaching – Julie is able to use the coaching process to help her develop the skills she needs to deal with group presentations. She attends her first session and while she expresses her anxiety about presenting to others she is willing and able to use a variety of techniques and strategies such as attending a presentation skills training course, using role-play and using coping imagery. The coach knows that Julie is benefiting from the coaching process due to the progress she makes. Each session builds on the last and while Julie finds some things harder than others to do she is able to develop her ability at group presentations.

Counselling – Julie finds her anxiety gets the better of her and that she is unable to use the strategies and techniques that would help her. Whatever the coach tries to do Julie ends up talking about how awful she feels. In her first session she is very anxious and tense. The coach decides to see if Julie could use a couple of basic strategies before the second session. When Julie arrives for the second session she has made no progress and continues to come across as extremely anxious. In this case the coach decides that coaching is not appropriate, discusses the limitations of the coaching process with Julie and suggests that counselling would be more appropriate. The coach then provides an appropriate referral source to Julie.

There will, of course, always be some clients who fall on the borderline between coaching and counselling and coaches will need to consider carefully whether what they can offer will be of real help to the client. In such instances it would be useful to talk to a coaching supervisor or respected colleague and/or share one's concern with the client. There is also the frequent situation where a client needs a counselling intervention in one area but is capable of gaining the full benefit from coaching elsewhere. The seasoned and broadly trained coach will be able to mix both types of intervention at will, but should retain a developmental approach to their clients. As a rule: 'if it ain't broke, don't fix it'.

There is a great temptation for therapists who may wish to become coaches to slip into the therapeutic relationship simply because the coach has the skills to do so. However, this way of working can have a downside, as a number of issues need to be taken into account. Firstly, the client and sponsoring organisation did not contract for counselling but for coaching and therefore the coach needs to consider the implications of changing the nature of the contract. Secondly, the coach needs to consider the time constraints of the coaching contract and whether the outcomes that were originally agreed can be met in this time by using a counselling approach. Thirdly, there are occasions when the client may become confused and lose the focus of what he or she is trying to achieve.

Referring clients

This is a short section because the message is simple:

- Have a referral network in place
- If in doubt, check with a supervisor immediately

Clinical referral

What do we mean by referring beyond the coaching/counselling discussion above? We define referring as those situations where the behaviour of a client is such that they could put themselves or others at risk. We also consider those situations where the business could be at risk or where illegal acts are taking place.

Early in his career, one of us had a client who was no longer 'live' but with whom he stayed in touch occasionally. At some stage, it became obvious that the client was stressed and disturbed, and was acting less and less coherently. The coach became suspicious and called a couple of clinical psychologists who rapidly diagnosed the early stages of a psychotic episode. The client was interned voluntarily and was able to resume a normal work life after he had been stabilised and the sources of extreme stress had been identified and addressed.

This is not a frequent example, but coaches should be prepared for such an occurrence. An article by Steven Berglas in the *Harvard Business Review* (2002) claimed that coaches should all be psychiatrists because there were so many cases of pathological narcissism in senior management. This is obviously an extreme and somewhat self-serving statement from the author, but it raises the need to have both alarm bells and a referral network. The coach should also resist the temptation to break confidentiality even when the sponsor (e.g. HR director) is a qualified psychologist. Currently, coaches are not subject to the same ethical guidelines and legal enforcement on the issue of confidentiality as the medical and psychological professions. As a reminder for non-psychologists, UK law is particularly strict on confidentiality and most referrals to clinicians go through general practitioners and are voluntary.

Business referral

If we accept that some clients may need the support of mental health practitioners, we should also consider that some might need 'company doctors'. First, there is the fairly straightforward case of suspected fraud or malpractice. We refer you to the section in this chapter concerning confidentiality and UK law. A more interesting case is when the client is out of their depth or out of time to carry out the business task that will enable them to achieve some personal development goals. Consider the following example:

> *Christopher has just been appointed to his first big senior management role. He has confidence issues concerning his ability to deliver and to build the team, particularly in the area of finance: his background is in marketing and he is not very numerate. He really needs to get 'behind the numbers' but requires help to build his skills in a confidential way: he believes that he should not allow himself to show any weakness in this new, highly visible role.*

Obviously, the business coach can deal comfortably with the confidence issues and perhaps reframe the beliefs around infallibility, but can they reasonably tackle financial analysis? Even if a coach is from a business background, are their skills and industry knowledge up to date? Our view is that well prepared business coaches will also have a network of management consultants and other experts to whom they can refer clients when they make the professional judgement that help is needed that they can't provide. Another issue is obviously the nature and limits of the coaching contract: even if the coach is capable of carrying out the analysis, there may be a need for a separate agreement for consulting services. In the example above, the coach was sufficiently experienced to develop a financial model together with the client but still called on an external modelling expert to confirm the robustness of the work. An interesting side benefit of this consulting intervention was that the model revealed some significant weaknesses in the finance director's judgement, at a time when the client was rebuilding his core team.

In conclusion: it's all about professionalism

This chapter has described what coaches should do to be better professionals. In doing so, they help the whole industry gain credibility: a clear 'win-win'.

First, business coaches need to limit their risk and make the outcome of their work explicit. They do this through formal contracts, as well as behavioural contracts. This immediately positions the coach as a serious supplier of services, on a par with other professionals such as accountants or consultants.

Second, coaches need to realise that the profession is in need of branding and tightening. This is what professional organisations are for, and the UK now has a good choice of extremely competent bodies.

Third, coaches' skills are a depreciating asset: the 30 hours of CPD are a strict minimum in our view and the best coaches maintain a permanent state of curiosity and learning.

Supervision provides a perfect platform to explore issues with colleagues and should be encouraged, if not made mandatory.

Finally, coaches are not superhuman: they need to understand their boundaries and be prepared to refer clients both to therapists and company doctors when needed.

Conclusions: the future of business coaching

We started this book by arguing that business coaching was in need of increased objectivity and in Chapter 7 we presented strong evidence of increased professionalism from all involved. Where does this take us next? In this final chapter we review what we have learnt and make predictions regarding the nature of the business coaching relationship and its content.

A strategic service that provides value for money

We examined coaching from many different angles and concluded that, when used shrewdly, coaching could be an extremely effective weapon in the war for talent and could provide sustainable competitive advantage. We also saw that there were many ways of measuring return on investment and that, even if you did not believe that magic equation of £1 spent = £6 saved, there was ample evidence of tangible and intangible benefits. Even the tightest-fisted finance director should approve of business coaching.

Now this is all true at a fairly senior level, but is it sufficient to create innovative and resilient organisations? We believe that the next wave of business coaching will drill down the organisation. There are already many examples of 'coaching the coaches' – i.e. training managers to behave in a coaching fashion with their staff, as well as 'mixed interventions' where coaches are brought in as part of a mixed curriculum.

A word in search of an identity . . . not a problem

Despite the extreme dilution of the term coaching, we found no Wild West situation: buyers of coaching are increasingly sophisticated and, although there is no obvious best practice, they make their own sensible rules and apply them purposefully.

We also found that clients were comfortable with the coaching process and did not care much about definitions. It was more important to them to know what was actually going to happen during the sessions and that confidentiality would be respected.

Our prediction is that coaching will remain a fairly loose term, very much like management consulting. Brands will emerge, but their power will be limited due to the very personalised relationship between coach and client. We may get to a situation similar to that of international law firms: the brand is strong, but star coaches will have a stronger client following than their firm.

Content vs. process: the need for explicit coaching frameworks

We have seen that business coaches need to be able to explain how they achieve change through their particular brand of coaching. They need to be able to demonstrate a process that has validity to a buyer. They do not all have, of course, to agree on what that process is. Although the process itself may not be immediately visible to the naked eye of the one being coached, it underlies and guides the coach's decisions about what to cover in order to facilitate the desired changes. More generally, business coaches need to recognise that their clients are intelligent, curious and informed.

We proposed our own frameworks: the ITEA model for content and the draw/achieve/motivate one for process. They are robust and proven. What should be remembered is the iterative nature of these frameworks: to use a business analogy, clients should not expect to treat the coaching process as a Gantt chart; it is more like a balanced score card, with many feedback loops and requiring constant tuning.

Going forward, we think that there will be an increased distinction between 'cookbook' coaching, which rests on sets of frameworks and acronyms as taught in weekend courses, and experienced professionals who can measure the impact of their interventions and have considerable flexibility in their approaches, within the context of a clear framework. It is not yet clear how this will translate in terms of supply segmentation, but professional organisations will probably have a role to play (see below).

Psychology works: a nice surprise?

We carried out a deep review of the best coaching 'technologies' and discovered that psychology as classically taught does not need to be thrown out in a business context; it actually works quite well, provided that the coach is credible in industry. We showed that our preferred approaches – cognitive-behavioural and positive psychology – work particularly well in business.

This review of coaching is particularly useful as a roadmap for all involved: what to look for when identifying competent coaches, what to study for the non-professional psychologist and also the eminently interesting discovery of the mechanisms of what makes business people tick.

Going forward, we think that business will eventually integrate the fact that coaching is a psychological process and that it can be applied systematically as a supporting, not a remedial, approach. It will take some time for the image of the bearded analyst and couch to disappear, but early movers will gain a competitive advantage. This may slant the purchasing towards psychologists or at least towards qualified non-psychologist coaches. This takes us back to the role of professional bodies. In all cases strong business credibility will remain essential.

Coaching business people: more than the alpha male

We examined three broad families of business applications: business personalities, business stages and business skills. The first referred to who we are and how we feel when in business. The second focused on career stages and how the nature of coaching interventions varies as we move from junior, specialised positions to more experienced ones. Finally, we looked at coaching as an effective way to plug gaps in the toolkit needed to succeed in business.

Beyond specific techniques, we drew two major conclusions: businesses will continue to need a wide spread of interventions and individual coaches cannot deliver all of them by themselves. This points to interesting developments in terms of industry structure: business coaches should have a clear awareness of their comfort zone and ally themselves with other experts to cover the whole gamut of business interventions. If coaches need to pool their skills, what will be the best format to do so: loose alliances or employment in large firms? We think that branded medium-sized firms are likely to prevail.

Sponsors will purchase more coaching, more wisely

We had the good fortune to interview five major multinational buyers of coaching and have candid conversations about what worked, how they were organised and how they measured success. This is highly relevant to HR professionals who want to compare notes, to coaches who want to offer more relevant services and to would-be coaches who can now refine their preparation.

Our conclusion was that HR buyers, and sometimes procurement departments, have largely taken over the purchase of coaching and that the time of 'private deals' between executive and coach is largely over. HR departments want to hand-pick their coaches and offer their internal clients a good choice of suppliers – sometimes internal coaches. This is a good thing in the sense that it brings coaching to the board table in an explicit and professional way, creating sustainability for our industry. It also means that coaches must become considerably wiser to the ways of business, particularly if they come from a counselling environment.

HR directors are key drivers in pushing coaching up and down the hierarchy and integrating it with other learning and development initiatives. To do this they need help: they want the profession to mature and demonstrate high ethics, clarity about what can be done and sound methodologies and approaches. Coaching should be purchased like other services, and a reasonable level of documentation of interventions and results should be created. The traditional 'big questions' of coaching such as return on investment or confidentiality come as less important than first expected and buyers deal with them pragmatically: coaches must be competent and professional, keep sight of the company's objectives, be priced within market boundaries and document their work.

Personal stories demonstrate the power of coaching

It was refreshing and insightful to peek behind the closed door and to get a personal account of coaching from real clients in a business context. It was also heartening to see the tremendous results achieved by these clients.

These personal stories demonstrated that businesspeople will seek coaching for very different reasons, but there are some universal themes: all were at a stage of intense personal questioning somehow related to self-perception, competence and relationship with others. It would have been easy to take a counselling approach and to 'find and cure a problem'. Instead the coaches used a wide range of skills and evidence to liberate their clients from constraining behaviours, perceptions and emotions and set them free to reach the next level in their careers. Those who were not already in transition by and large stayed in their business and made an impact on their relationship with others, often becoming staff coaches themselves and basically more mature managers.

It was interesting to note that the process was not always pleasant, particularly at the beginning: ambiguity is always difficult to deal with, particularly at first. The coaches' use of objective data coupled with a supportive yet impartial attitude helped tremendously. Some of the discomfort came from the realisation that work and life could not be separated that easily and that they had to investigate the causes of emotions and behaviour beyond the relatively secure four walls of the business.

Going forward, we think that businesses will be less scared of tackling a broad agenda but will respect its confidentiality. They will also be aware that coaching has to be more than an emotional blanket and that outcomes will need to be quite specific. This will increase pressure on the coach regarding confidentiality, agenda boundaries and limits of competence.

Use all the tools available to increase professionalism

By now the agenda has become quite clear: everybody involved in the coaching industry wants to increase professionalism. The same way coaches move their clients from awareness to action, we spent some time on an essential set of actions for business coaches: what do they need to do to raise their professionalism?

We found that, at a minimum, they need to have a clear approach to contracting – including confidentiality – in order to become serious suppliers to businesses. Like all suppliers of services to large companies, they need to manage their risk and be explicit about what they will deliver. We proposed an example of a behavioural contract that can be adapted to any situation.

In addition to demonstrating a clear approach to the coaching process, coaches also need to show that they are taking their own development and practice seriously: continual professional development, supervision and affiliation are becoming important in the eyes of the buyer, particularly for those coaches not from a psychology background.

An interesting element of professionalisation is the ability to recognise boundaries and refer clients. This is well established in other professions and we think that the aptitude to navigate between coaching and counselling, to make contractual boundaries explicit and to have occasional access to clinical practitioners as well as management consultants will be a differentiating feature of good business coaches.

In conclusion: the future is bright!

When we set out to write this book we had mixed feelings: on the one hand we knew that coaching works and that it provides tremendous value to clients and sponsors; but were we the only ones to know? We were also concerned that coaching had lost its way. Actually we still think that there a prize for whoever comes up with a distinctive name to describe the section of our profession that helps create tremendous competitive advantage in business organisations.

Twelve months later we are considerably more optimistic: clients and sponsors see a clear benefit to coaching, we can identify what constitutes best practice at all levels, and all participants in the industry are pushing for increased professionalism. We see a specific agenda for all involved:

- Buyers and sponsors have an increased data set from which to demonstrate the benefits of coaching. They are becoming clearer about the role, positioning and frequency of coaching interventions. Their challenge is to make coaching stick in the boardroom and demonstrate its competitive advantage.

- Clients are gradually being freed from the old 'there must be something wrong with me' stigma and are using coaching as a regular developmental intervention at various stages in their careers. Their challenge is to use their newly-acquired skills to coach others and to permeate the organisation with a coaching ethos.

- Practitioners and would-be coaches now understand that the industry will polarise between occasional business helpers – be they mentors or counsellors – and full-time professionals who constantly develop both sides of their competence: business and psychology. They need to decide if they want to embrace the challenge of increased professionalism.

- Coaching firms now realise that they are unlikely to become global businesses but that a clear offering and robust processes are essential to long-term success. They need to invest in research, branding, quality assurance and recruitment. Their challenge is not going to be cut-throat competition or margin pressure, but differentiation.

- Coaching organisations have a clear challenge: to be both inclusive of psychologists and business people, and to provide stringent qualifications so as to raise professionalism. The UK model is inherently more anarchic and ambiguous than the Continental one which typically focuses more on rules, regulations and barriers to entry. This means that some consolidation between various organisations should be expected. May the best one win!

All of this points to a very dynamic industry going in the 'right' direction. In other words, the future is bright!

Appendices

These appendices are referred to in the main text of the book and should be of help to coaches seeking for structure, sponsors who want to professionalise their purchases of coaching services and clients who want a more formal understanding of the coaching process.

They comprise the following:

- Appendix 1 – coaching pack
- Appendix 2 – selected Association for Coaching guidelines
- Appendix 3 – behavioural contract elements

Appendix 1: coaching pack

Excellent coaching is backed by a high standard of efficient record-keeping, ensuring accurate feedback, effective use of supervision time, quality control and general administrative efficiency. This basic pack covers data collection, records of coaching sessions, progress review and a supervision preparation checklist. Most coaches will wish to supplement these and develop their own system to maintain their professional standards.

Data collection

Company name		Sector
Name of sponsor		Job title
Name of client		Job title
Dates of meetings	1	4
No. of sessions agreed	2	5
	3	6
Reasons for coaching		
Issues in the organisation		
Initial goals		
Review dates		

Record of coaching sessions

Coach		Company	
Client			
Start date			

Date and coaching session no.	
Summary of session	
Key client tools introduced	
Tasks for next session	

Progress review

Coach	
Date of review	
No. of sessions	
Original development issue	
Intervention	
What did the client think had been achieved?	
What did the coach think had been achieved?	
Future development for client	
Follow-up	
Referrals?	

Supervision preparation

Name of coach	
Date of supervision	
Number of coaching sessions since last supervision	1 2 3 4 5 6 Other . . .
Presenting issue	
Summary of progress	
Anything which may be hindering progress	
Coach's feelings about the case	
Coach's needs in supervision	
Outcome of supervision	

Appendix 2: Association for Coaching guidelines

Coaching definitions

Coaching

Coaching enables the client to be the best they can be in the areas they choose to focus on.

Typically the client meets with the coach in a one-to-one confidential partnership. The client chooses the focus of the conversation and the coach works with them by listening and contributing observations and questions to help them clarify their understanding of the situation and move them into action to progress towards their goals. (The client brings the content; the coach provides a process, which can apply in any context.)

Coaching accelerates the client's progress by helping them to focus on where they want to go, become aware of blocks, attitudes and aptitudes that affect their choices and by supporting them in developing strategies to achieve their goals. Ownership of content and decisions remains with the client throughout.

There are a number of terms used in coaching and we seek to define them below.

Corporate coaching

This variation of the coaching relationship can be likened to coaching a football team. The coach has the interests of the whole team at heart and is seeking to support the team to achieve its goals. For the team to achieve its goals, each of the players and other members must be aligned to the team goals, and their own goals must be in tune with them. The coach may work with individuals in the team to support them to achieve their goals and/or may work with the whole team to support it in achieving its goals.

The corporate coach has the corporate goals at heart and may work with individuals or teams within the organisation to support them in achieving the goals. Corporate coaches need to have an understanding of the operational dimensions of the organisation, although they will focus on the two elements of people and leadership.

Executive coaching is a subset of corporate coaching and focuses on the executive. Executive coaching may be synonymous with leadership coaching in that executive coaching is typically with the more senior members or leaders of the organisation.

Business coaching

The difference between 'corporate' and 'business' coaching is the size of the organisation involved *and also the type of support from the coach*. Business coaching is typically one-to-one coaching with business owners or managers; the focus of the coaching is the success of the business, which is usually dependent on the performance of the business owner/manager. Typically the business coach will have experience in business and will take the role of a mentor, offering guidance and advice as well as using coaching skills to help the business owner/manager identify solutions.

Where clients need specific expertise (e.g. financial management), the coach will help them to identify suitable sources of that expertise; in some cases the coach will have the required expertise and can offer the knowledge and expertise as a consultant.

Executive coaching (leadership coaching)

Here the coach works with the executive (or high potential manager) as above in the generic definition of coaching. The coach is committed to the executive's goals. It is the responsibility of the executive and the organisation to ensure that their goals are aligned.

For example, this may involve working within specific areas of leadership development, such as assessment of their leadership style, talents and vision and/or in skill development areas, such as time management, confidence, impact and influence, and leading change. Additionally, the coach can provide an external support system that encourages the executive to deal with the challenges that may arise from change within an organisation.

Psychological coaching

Psychological coaching is a tool used to help clients overcome psychological blocks. It is used as a coaching tool as and when necessary in all types of coaching situations. Forms of psychological coaching include, for example, cognitive-behavioural coaching (CBC) and neuro-linguistic programming (NLP). Psychological coaching should only be performed by appropriately qualified coaches and clear boundaries should be agreed at contract stage.

Group coaching or team coaching

Here the coaching methodology is used for teams and team development, for example with functional teams or peer groups. Group coaching may address specific processes with the team (e.g. problem-solving, decision-making, communication etc.).

Specific coaching

Here the coach offers their services in a context they have expertise in (e.g. career, health, stress management or outplacement). The coaching process is similar to coaching in that the ownership remains with the client, *and* the coach often has a proven process for this particular focus and permission to offer information, guidance and advice.

Mentoring

In the mentoring relationship the client seeks out an individual with more relevant experience who will help fast-track the client through the organisation/industry/profession. The mentor will give advice within the context based on their experience and the relationship is typically ongoing over a long period of time. Mentoring uses some of the same skills as coaching and the process is similar, except that the individual receives guidance from the mentor. The relationship is one of the experienced person passing on knowledge and skills to the individual, who accepts these and decides what to use to help in their own situation. The focus of attention is more on the mentor passing on their wisdom, although based on the individual's agenda.

Counselling

Typically an individual will seek a professional counsellor when they experience blockage, due to past experiences, preventing them moving forward. The counsellor works one-to-one with the individual to identify the causes of the blockage and help them come to terms with it and thereby prepare them to move on. Professional counsellors deal with personal issues in much greater depth than would generally be the case in coaching. Counselling should only be performed by appropriately qualified counsellors and clear boundaries should be agreed at contract stage.

Consulting

The consulting relationship varies enormously. Consultants work on behalf of the organisation and are called in due to their experience of the situation the organisation faces. Typically the consultant will give advice and/or provide processes that the organisation can use to short-cut the route to their goal and benefit from the learning of the consultant. This service is typically provided one-to-many and the consultant is working for the organisation rather than the individual.

Quality standards

These quality points are designed to help clients choose an appropriate coach and to help new coaches identify what is important to clients.

Fit for the client's purpose

The client first has to decide what they want from a coach. The process of choosing a coach will help the client clarify what they can gain from coaching and what the coaching process involves.

Developing an effective coach/client relationship

It's important that the client selects a coach they have confidence in and can work honestly with.

Typically the first session is one where client and coach get to know each other and can test that both feel they can work well together to achieve the client's goals. A coaching relationship involves both support and challenge from the coach, and the client needs to feel comfortable enough with the coach to accept this.

How will quality be tested in this relationship?

The client needs to identify the clear outcomes they expect from the coaching. These could include numerical targets (e.g. improved team sales), or qualitative criteria (e.g. more positive feedback on teamworking). If the client knows they have an issue to resolve through coaching and is not sure exactly what the outcomes should be, the first session with the coach can be used to define objectives. Additionally, the quality of the relationship and how coach and client are working together counts to the likely success.

Indicators of effective coaching technique include:

- Does the coach listen well, are they supportive and non-judgemental yet challenging?
- Does the coach help the client to understand their situation and find their own solutions?
- Does the client feel they are in control?

Experience, background, training and professional qualifications

Coaches come from a range of professional backgrounds including personnel, psychology, management, training, management consulting, counselling, health and therapy. Look for experience and background that show the coach has previously worked with the issues and challenges the client wants to bring to coaching. In many cases experience of a specific industry is less relevant than the breadth of experience a coach can bring to the challenge.

Coaches use different models and philosophies of coaching. The client may want to ask the coach what model they use and how it is suitable for addressing their current requirement. For the client, knowing that the coach works to a useful model that they can understand is a reflection of the coach's quality.

Professional memberships and supervision

A coach should belong to at least one association that indicates they are working to certain ethical and professional standards and maintaining their continuing professional development (CPD). The coach should be able to show you a copy of the standards that they are adhering to.

The coach may participate in co-coaching and/or supervision to support their learning and quality standards. This is a strong indicator that the coach takes their professionalism seriously and is seeking to maintain high-quality standards.

Testimonials and references
(evidence of success)

If the client is still in doubt about the credibility of the coach, the coach should be able to provide references and testimonials from previous clients. However, it must be acknowledged that each coaching relationship is individual and testimonials are essentially only evidence that the coach has experience.

Relationships and commitments

The following is an extensive description of all relationships between all parties involved in a coaching contract. See diagram on page 163 for a map of relationships.

Responsibility	Coach	Client	Organisation
Goals	Committed to client's goals and supports them to ensure alignment	Sets goals aligned with organisation *and* with personal needs	Agrees goals with client and ensures fit with organisational goals
Learning/ change	Provides the process to help client change. Maintains own knowledge and skills at high standard to offer client most effective methods of change	Wants to learn and change and is committed to the process	Wants to help client learn and change, and supports implementation
Confidentiality	Keeps confidentiality on personal issues and respects the organisation's non-disclosure agreement	Keeps organisational confidentiality as appropriate, shares information in confidence as they prefer	Does not ask for confidential information
Presence	Attends all sessions promptly and ready	Arrives on time and prepared for all sessions	Makes it possible for client to attend sessions
Plan	Develops appropriate plan with the client, agrees budget, outcomes and timing with organisation	Commits to plan of learning and change	Agrees outline plan and budget with coach and client
Respect	Respects client and organisation and is non-judgemental	Respects coach and organisation	Respects client and coach

continued

Responsibility	Coach	Client	Organisation
Measures	Agrees where client is now and measures for growth/goal achievement with client	Agrees current position and measures for growth with coach and in outline with organisation	Agrees measures/ evidence for progress with client
Ownership	Coach helps client with process	Client makes decisions, owns the results and takes responsibility for own behaviours	Accepts client decisions and makes organisation's decisions
Environment	Creates learning environment for client in the sessions	Establishes goals and seeks change within their control	Creates no-blame environment so client can address issues and make mistakes as part of the learning
Relationship	Builds rapport with client and members of the organisation. Establishes permission-based working relationship with client	Develops open and honest working relationship with coach and facilitates contact with other members of the organisation as appropriate	Creates effective working relationship with coach as needed to support client and maintains open and honest relationship with client

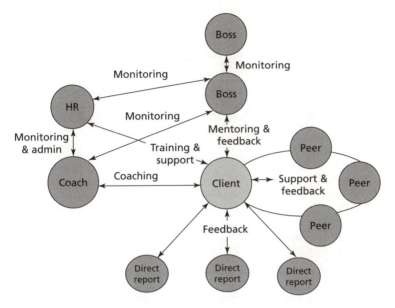

Comprehensive picture of reporting relationships

Source: Courtesy of A. Caillet, © President Leaders LLC, 2004

Coaching evaluation form

PART ONE

How do you rate your coach on the following variables covering skills, techniques and attributes?

A How good was your coach at . . . (1 = low – 5 = high)

1 Keeping agreed appointments   1 2 3 4 5

2 Allowing you to set the agenda for your sessions   1 2 3 4 5

3 Keeping a check on the points agreed during your sessions and feeding these back to you including reviewing points from previous sessions   1 2 3 4 5

4 Encouraging you to use a log or reflection note
to reflect on learning experiences   1 2 3 4 5

5 Sharing experiences and ideas as options for you
to consider   1 2 3 4 5

B   How well did your coach . . . (1 = low – 5 = high)

6 Establish rapport with you – listening to what
you said and displaying empathy with your
thoughts and ideas, giving clear responses
and summaries, communicating openly with
you etc.   1 2 3 4 5

7 Explain clearly any necessary concepts,
information and techniques giving clear,
concise and constructive feedback   1 2 3 4 5

8 Use questionnaires and/or self-assessment
profiles (if appropriate) to help you understand
yourself better   1 2 3 4 5

9 Ensure you retained responsibility to solve
problems and change your behaviour, gaining
your commitment to a personal action plan   1 2 3 4 5

C   How good was your coach at . . . (1 = low – 5 = high)

10 Asserting themselves without being aggressive
or passive   1 2 3 4 5

11 Showing that they were knowledgeable,
skilful and willing to liaise with other appropriate
experts   1 2 3 4 5

12 Demonstrating good time management
practices   1 2 3 4 5

13 Communicating a genuine belief in the potential for people to improve their performance   1 2 3 4 5

14 Managing your emotions   1 2 3 4 5

15 Acting as a good role model   1 2 3 4 5

D How good was the coaching programme at helping you to . . . (1 = low – 5 = high)

16 Assess your current levels of competence   1 2 3 4 5

17 Improve your performance   1 2 3 4 5

18 Become more aware of learning   1 2 3 4 5

19 Prioritise your development needs   1 2 3 4 5

20 Maximise any learning opportunities   1 2 3 4 5

21 Set yourself development goals or targets   1 2 3 4 5

22 Monitor and/or evaluate the achievement of your objectives   1 2 3 4 5

23 Set yourself new goals   1 2 3 4 5

24 Create a personal development plan   1 2 3 4 5

25 Feel more positive about your development   1 2 3 4 5

26 Raise your morale   1 2 3 4 5

PART TWO

All development initiatives should deliver some business benefits. How well did you think the coaching programme worked from this point of view? Answer as many of the following questions as possible.

Please indicate your level of agreement with each of the following statements (1 = strongly disagree; 3 = neither agree nor disagree; 5 = strongly agree; n/a = not applicable)

1   The provision of coaching demonstrates to me that this company/organisation cares about my development   1 2 3 4 5 n/a

2   I believe that the coaching I have received has had a direct beneficial impact upon the business/work in my area   1 2 3 4 5 n/a

3   My motivation has increased as a result of the coaching   1 2 3 4 5 n/a

4   My coaching has helped me sort out personal issues which may otherwise have affected my performance at work   1 2 3 4 5 n/a

5   I am more likely to stay with the company/ organisation as a result of receiving coaching   1 2 3 4 5 n/a

6   It would not be difficult for me to demonstrate how coaching has improved my personal performance at work   1 2 3 4 5 n/a

7   My performance at work has definitely been enhanced as a result of my coaching   1 2 3 4 5 n/a

8   My coaching has *directly* resulted in business benefits   1 2 3 4 5 n/a

9   My coaching has *indirectly* resulted in business benefits   1 2 3 4 5 n/a

PART THREE

How far did your coach help you to reach your agreed outcome measurements?

Identify your outcome targets and then indicate agreement (1 = low – 5 = high)

1   1 2 3 4 5
2   1 2 3 4 5
3   1 2 3 4 5

Are there any other personal or business benefits you believe have been derived from your coaching?

Please add any further comments

Please adapt this form to your needs in evaluating coaching programmes in your organisation and in providing feedback to the coaches.

Appendix 3: behavioural contract elements

Objectives and outcomes (examples)

The process is to list objectives as general statements, and then make them specific in terms of observable behaviours.

Coaching objectives required

1 Communicate more effectively.
2 Feel more confident.
3 . . .
4 . . .

Outcomes

1 To organise regular weekly staff briefing.
2 To improve my ability to be assertive by using techniques such as the three-step model used in assertiveness training. To provide examples of when and where this technique has been used.
3 To use the in-house magazine to inform other people in the organisation of the work that the department is doing.
4 . . .
5 . . .

Confidentiality and feedback

Confidentiality

It is worth being specific, even if only to remind all concerned about the legal context: 'Whilst recognising the need for discretion and confidentiality, all parties agree to take into account all aspects relating to the law and duty of care'.

Feedback

It is worth specifying feedback procedures as per the following examples:

1 A meeting between all parties to take place at mid-point in the coaching process either in person or via the telephone.
2 To provide a written report at the end of the coaching process agreed with the client.

Sign off

Remember to include a form of contract that allows for all three parties to sign off, even if behavioural contract meetings take place two-by-two.

Bibliography

Adler, N.J. (2001) *International Dimensions Of Organizational Behaviour*. Boston, MA: South Western College Publishing.

Adler, N.J. and Izraeli, D.N. (eds) (1994) *Competitive Frontiers: Women Managers in a Global Economy*. Cambridge, MA: Blackwell Publishers.

Bandler, R. and Grinder, J. (1975) *The Structure of Magic*. Los Altos, CA: Science and Behavior Books.

Beck, A. (1976) *Cognitive Therapy and the Emotional Disorders*. New York: International Universities Press.

Blanchard, K. and Johnson, S. (2004) *The One Minute Manager*. London: HarperCollins Business.

Blanchard, K. and Shula, D. (1995) *Everyone's a Coach*. New York: Harper Business.

Berglas, S. (2002) The very real dangers of executive coaching, *Harvard Business Review*, June, 86–92.

Caplan, J. (2003) *Coaching for the Future*. London: CIPD.

Carroll, M. (1996) *Counselling Supervision*. London: Cassell.

Cole, S.A. and Bird, J.(2000) *The Medical Interview*. Saint Louis, MO: Mosby.

Dilts, R. (1998) *Modeling with NLP*. Capitola, CA: Meta Publications.

Egan, G. (1990) *The Skilled Helper: A Systematic Approach to Effective Helping*. Belmont, CA: Brooks/Cole Publishing Company.

Ellis, A. and Grieger, R. (1977) *Handbook of Rational-emotive Therapy*. New York: Springer.

Gallwey, T. (1974) *The Inner Game of Tennis*. New York: Random House.

Grant, A.M. and Palmer, S. (2002) 'Coaching psychology'. Meeting held at the annual conference of Division of Counselling Psychology, British Psychological Society, Torquay, 18 May.

Hemp, P. (2004) Presenteeism: at work – but out of it, *Harvard Business Review*, October, 49–58.

Jarvis, J. (2004) *Coaching and Buying Coaching Services*. London: CIPD.

Landsberg, M. (1997) *The Tao of Coaching*. London: HarperCollins Business.

Lawley, J. and Tompkins, P. (2000) *Metaphors in Mind*. London: The Developing Company Press.

McDermott, I. and Jago, W. (2001) *The NLP Coach*. London: Piatkus.

Neenan, M. and Dryden, W. (2002) *Life Coaching: A Cognitive Behavioural Approach*. London: Brunner-Routledge.

Peltier, B. (2001) *The Psychology of Executive Coaching*. Ann Arbor, MI: Taylor & Francis.

Peterson, C. and Seligman, M.E.P. (2004) *Character Strengths and Virtues*. New York: Oxford University Press.

Prochaska, J.O. and DiClemente, C.C. (1982) Transtheoretical therapy: towards a more integrative model of change, *Psychotherapy: Theory, Research and Practice*, 19: 276–88.

Proctor, B. and Inskipp, F. (1988) *Skills for Supervising and Being Supervised*. St Leonards on Sea: Alexia Publications.

Rogers, C. (1958) The characteristics of a helping relationship, *Personnel and Guidance Journal*, 37(1): 6–16.

Rogers, C. (1961) The characteristics of a helping relationship, in C. Rogers, *On Becoming A Person: A Therapist's View of Psychotherapy*. New York: Houghton Mifflin.

Seligman, M. (1991) *Learned Optimism*. New York: Knopf.

Seligman, M. (2003) *Authentic Happiness*. London: Nicholas Brealey Publishing.

Skiffington, S. and Zeus, P. (2003) *Behavioral Coaching: How to Build Sustainable Personal and Organisational Strength*. Sydney: McGraw Hill.

Spencer, L. (2004) *The Diversity Pocketbook*. Management Pocket Books.

Watson, D., Clark, L.A. and Tellegen, A. (1988) Development and validation of brief measures of positive and negative affect: the PANAS scales, *Journal of Personality and Social Psychology*, 54: 1063–70.

West, L. and Milan, M. (2001) *The Reflecting Glass: Professional Coaching for Leadership Development*. UK: Palgrave.

Whitmore, J. (2002) *Coaching for Performance*. London: Nicholas Brealey Publishing.

Whitworth, L., Kimsey-House, H. and Sandahl, P. (1998) *Co-Active Coaching*. Palo Alto, CA: Davies-Black Publishing.

William, P. and Davis, D. (2002) *Therapist as Life Coach: Transforming your Practice*. USA: Norton & Co.

Index